D0975138

WITHIN REACH

Robert L. Millet

Deseret Book Company
Salt Lake City, Utah

Library of Congress Cataloging-in-Publication Data

Millet, Robert L.
  Within reach / Robert L. Millet.
     p.   cm.
  Includes bibliographical references and indexes.
  ISBN 0-87579-968-X
     1. Perfection—Religious aspects—Mormon Church.
  2. Mormon Church—Doctrines. 3. Church of Jesus Christ of Latter-day Saints—Doctrines. I. Title.
  BX8643.P47M55   1995
  234—dc20   95-7681
                                                               CIP

Printed in the United States of America

10   9   8   7   6   5   4   3   2   1

Wherefore, if ye shall press forward, feasting upon the word of Christ, and endure to the end, behold, thus saith the Father: Ye shall have eternal life.

—2 NEPHI 31:20

If thou wilt do good, yea, and hold out faithful to the end, thou shalt be saved in the kingdom of God, which is the greatest of all the gifts of God; for there is no gift greater than the gift of salvation.

—D&C 6:13

CONTENTS

PREFACE

On one occasion Jesus set forth the sobering principle that it is easier for a camel to go through the eye of a needle than for a man or woman who trusts in riches to enter into the kingdom of God. "When his disciples heard it, they were exceedingly amazed, saying, Who then can be saved?" (Matthew 19:24–25).

Indeed, who *can* be saved? Or rather, who *will* be saved? Are there but few who will make it? Is heaven reserved for the prophets and the little children who died before the age of accountability? Will the bulk of humankind fall short of the glory of God and spend an eternity racked with the gnashing realization of what could have been? And what of the Latter-day Saints? How many will be exalted? On the other hand, how many will receive the gospel, participate in the ordinances of salvation, and then qualify for something less than eternal life?

These are questions I have pondered for many years. In our efforts to assure faithful endurance to the end, we speak frequently of the difficulty of navigating the strait and narrow path and of the dangers associated with the precarious climb to celestial glory. In our eagerness to maintain a tight grip on the iron rod, we focus on the justice of God, on the immutable decree that the Holy One "cannot look upon sin with the least degree of allowance" (D&C 1:31), and on the proclamation that "no unclean thing can enter into his kingdom" (3 Nephi 27:19). I suppose that such teachings do much to keep us in line and to plant in our hearts the fear of God's wrath and the torment of disappointment that will surely follow on the heels of missed opportunities. It is no doubt the case that occasionally nothing brings people to repentance "save it [be] exceeding harshness, preaching and prophesying . . . , and continually reminding [the Saints] of death, and the duration of eternity, and the judgments and the power of God, and all these things—stirring them up continually to keep them in the fear of the Lord." That is, those in authority must often use "exceedingly great plainness of speech" in order to keep the people "from going down speedily to destruction" (Enos 1:23).

And yet the gospel of Jesus Christ is good news, news that is intended to liberate us, lift our spirits, and lighten our burdens; it is the glad tidings "that he came into the world, even Jesus, to be crucified for the world, and to bear the sins of the world, and to sanctify the world, and to cleanse it from all unrighteousness; that through him all might be saved whom the Father had put into his power and made by him" (D&C 76:41–42). The gospel is the "power of God unto salvation" (Romans 1:16), a supernal power that leads to the peaceful assurance that we can make it. No one of us is outside the pale of saving mercy and grace; there is room in heaven for every person who believes in Christ, enters into covenant with him, and does his or her best to keep that covenant.

Joseph Smith penetrated the veil and opened the heavens. He saw God and Jesus Christ. In the process, he came to know something of everlasting import: that the Almighty God is in very deed our Heavenly Parent, the Father of our spirits, that he loves us perfectly and completely, and that he yearns to bless us here and exalt us hereafter. Through his Only Begotten Son he has made available the very powers of godliness, enabling us as mortals not only to be *with* God once again, but also to be *like* him. Nothing would bring our Eternal Father greater happiness than for his children to return to that divine presence they once enjoyed. Such knowledge fosters hope; it engenders joy and rejoicing.

In a modern revelation the Lord explained through the Prophet Joseph Smith that the gifts of the Spirit "are given for the benefit of those who love me and keep all my commandments, *and him that seeketh so to do*" (D&C 46:9; emphasis added). In that same book of scripture we are instructed: "If thou wilt do good, yea, and hold out faithful to the end, thou shalt be saved in the kingdom of God, which is the greatest of all the gifts of God; for *there is no gift greater than the gift of salvation*" (D&C 6:13; emphasis added). The transcendent blessings of exaltation in the celestial kingdom will come not to those who were perfect and absolutely free from sin in this life, for only Jesus our Savior would qualify according to that high standard. Rather, those who are bound for glory are those who do their best, who try their hardest, who learn to repent quickly and honestly, who learn to pray as if everything depended on the Lord and work as if everything depended on the Lord! Jesus Christ is the Hope of Israel. He is our Savior. As we learn to trust in and rely on his mighty arm, he will deliver us from death and sin and place eternal life within our reach. Of this I testify. For this I am immeasurably grateful.

IN THE PREPARATION OF THIS WORK I am indebted to many people—students, teachers, friends, and faculty colleagues—who have challenged me in my study to stretch and reach for deeper understanding. I express special thanks to Lori Soza, a capable and conscientious secretary and assistant, who has done much to prepare the manuscript of this book for publication. The nucleus of this book was an address delivered to the religious education faculty at Brigham Young University entitled "Are You a Saved Mormon?" Feedback in terms of suggestions, corrections, and broadened perspective were enthusiastically offered and gratefully received. Specifically, Professors Larry E. Dahl and Randy L. Bott provided the needed stimulus and valuable references. I thank Sheri Dew and Ronald Millett from Deseret Book for their encouragement to expand the talk into a short book, and Jay Parry for his keen and helpful editorial eye. In spite of so much help from others, however, I alone am responsible for the conclusions drawn from the evidence cited; this book is a private endeavor and not an official publication of either The Church of Jesus Christ of Latter-day Saints or Brigham Young University.

W HEN I WAS FIRST ORDAINED and set apart as a bishop in 1980, the stake president gave me a remarkable blessing. He offered wise and sound counsel, but none was more meaningful than the words, "Give to the people of your ward a vision of eternal life. Help them know they can make it."

Since that time I have served in numerous capacities in the Church, including three stake presidencies and again as bishop. I have become painfully aware of sin and error, of serious and soul-threatening mistakes of judgment, and of the agony and alienation known only to those who have left the strait and narrow path and lost the light they once had. I have witnessed families torn apart by self-

Prologue

ishness, pride, and abuse. I have looked on almost helplessly as individual Latter-day Saints have chosen to follow alternate voices, leave the fellowship of the Church, and in time become enemies to that which they once loved. I have labored for long hours with members who have struggled with issues of morality, the Word of Wisdom, or tithing.

And yet amid it all, the commission of my beloved leader—"Give to the people a vision of eternal life"—comes back to my mind again and again. They are haunting words, words that point up the need to have hope, to rejoice, to hold on in spite of difficulties and distress. I do think we can make it, make it to the celestial kingdom, make it to where God and Christ are. We cannot go there unclean or while harboring un-repentant sins, but I have complete confidence that through the person and powers of our Savior we can put off our sins, put on Christ, and become a people of promise. In the words of President Howard W. Hunter, "We must know Christ better than we know him; we must remember him more often than we remember him; we must serve him more valiantly than we serve him. Then we will drink water springing up unto eternal life and will eat the bread of life" (*That We Might Have Joy*, p. 5).

ARE WE QUALIFIED FOR THE CELESTIAL KINGDOM?

I tried as a bishop to provide this vision to the members of my ward, and I have tried to do the same thing since then with students, neighbors, and family members. Many times while in temple recommend inter-views, I have taken occasion to teach a lesson that I think has had an impact on at least some of my brothers and sisters. Let me set the scene. After all of the questions had been asked and answered properly, I frequently said: "Now, Brother (or Sister) Scott, you have done well. You have given the right answers to the questions I have been asked to pose to members of the Church before they go into the temple. You're fine. You can go to the temple. Now, off the record, just between you and me, let me ask you one final question: If you were to die this minute, drop dead right here in the office, and you were allowed to skip the spirit world experience, where would you go? What kingdom of glory would you qualify for?" After they sensed I was serious, that I sincerely wanted them to ponder the answer to my query, at least seven out of ten persons would sheepishly respond: "I don't know. I suppose the terrestrial kingdom?"

Then, if it seemed appropriate, I would push them a little. I would come back with, "Brother Scott, have you been lying to me?"

He would get a horrified look on his face and say: "Lying? Me? No, Bishop, why do you say that?"

"Brother Scott, do you really live the law of chastity, or have you been unfaithful to your wife and family?"

"Bishop," he would answer, "I really am trying to be morally clean."

"Then you must be lying about the Word of Wisdom or tithing. John, are you misrepresenting your financial situation before the Lord?"

"Heavens no, Bishop," he would say. "I honestly and faithfully pay my tithing."

"Then let me get this straight," I would say.

"You have a testimony of God, Christ, and the Holy Ghost. You have a witness of the truthfulness of the restored gospel and sustain the leadership of the Church. You live the law of chastity and the Word of Wisdom, and you are seeking to be honest in your dealings with your fellow beings. You are striving to keep your temple covenants. But you plan to go to the terrestrial kingdom?"

> NO ONE HAS BEEN SENT TO EARTH WHO DOES NOT HAVE THE CAPACITY TO RETURN TO GOD HONORABLY.

"Well, it's not that I plan to go there," the member would say. "It's just probably where I will end up."

"Why will you end up in the terrestrial kingdom?" I then inquired.

The answer, nine times out of ten, was as follows: "Well, Bishop, I'm not perfect. I make mistakes."

And then came the moment that mattered—a sacred teaching moment. "Brother Scott," I would say, gently but firmly, "I know you are not perfect and that you make mistakes. You are mortal. You are human. But I know also that you are trying to keep your covenants, not only with deeds but with your whole heart. You truly love God and want to please him. You qualify to hold a temple recommend. These are not things to be dismissed lightly. They place you in a remarkable minority in this world. They are an indication to you, to me, and to your Heavenly Father that you are on course, that you are on the path. At the end of that path is eternal life. Hold on. Hope on. We're going to make it."

RESISTING THE PULL OF DISCOURAGEMENT

Isn't such an approach risky? Aren't there those in the Church who will take advantage of this line of reasoning and then seek to rationalize their indifference, negligence, and even disobedience? Yes, I suppose there will always be those who want to take license in gospel liberty. But I feel keenly that there is a greater risk: that those who are really trying to do their best but falling short will yield to discouragement and conclude that they are simply not cut out for eternal glory. Bruce C. Hafen has written: "The person most in need of understanding the Savior's mercy is probably one who has worked himself to exhaustion in a sincere effort to repent, but who still believes his estrangement from God is permanent and hopeless. . . . I sense that an increasing number of deeply committed Church members are weighed down beyond the breaking point with discouragement about their personal lives. When we habitually understate the meaning of the Atonement, we take more serious risks than simply leaving one another without comforting reassurances—for some may simply drop out of the race, worn out and beaten down with the harsh and untrue belief that they are just not celestial material" (*The Broken Heart,* pp. 5–6).

In short, if Satan cannot get us to throw it all away through massive sin, or if he cannot make subtle but serious inroads against our character through his unrelenting assaults on goodness and decency, then perhaps he will tempt us to conclude things about ourselves that simply are not true—that we are somehow spiritually deficient, defective, or even depraved. Our attitude becomes one of: "I have tried and tried and tried to be perfect and I just can't do it. Why worry about it anymore? I quit!"

These are lies, vicious lies, spawned by the father of lies. To be sure, we can't do it alone, by ourselves, but with divine assistance and through a careful reexamination of how far we have already come, along with a rethinking of the truths pertaining to salvation and eternal life, we can reach the point where we have hope, what the scriptures call "hope in Christ" (see, for example, 1 Corinthians 15:19 and Jacob 2:19). That hope is more, far more, than willy-nilly wishing for happiness in the great beyond; it is a peaceful assurance, a sweet expectation, and a grand anticipation here of eternal reward hereafter, all because of our active and living faith in Jesus Christ.

No one has been sent to earth to fail. No one has come into this second estate who does not have the capacity to return to God honorably and, with him, enjoy peace and glory everlastingly. We simply must keep our bearings, keep our eyes on the Light and the Life, keep ourselves focused on the promise and hope of exaltation. Like Simon Peter, who walked on the water, we are able to defy the odds, accomplish the miraculous, and navigate the strait and narrow without permanent detour only when we keep our eyes riveted on Jesus Christ. In the words of a modern prophet, "It is my firm belief that if, as individual people, as families, communities, and nations, we could, like Peter, fix our eyes on Jesus, we too might walk triumphantly over the swelling waves of disbelief and remain unterrified amid the rising winds of doubt. But if we turn away our eyes from him in whom we must believe, as it is so easy to do and the world is so much tempted to do, if we look to the power and fury of those terrible and destructive elements around us rather than to him who can help and save us, then we shall inevitably sink in a sea of conflict and sorrow and despair.

"At such times when we feel the floods are threatening to drown us and the deep is going to swallow up the tossed vessel of our faith, I pray we may always hear amid the storm and the darkness that sweet utterance of the Savior of the world: 'Be of good cheer; it is I; be not afraid' (Matt. 14:27)" (Howard W. Hunter, *That We Might Have Joy*, p. 20).

Christ is our only hope, our way back to the safe harbor. Because of who he is and what he has done, there is no obstacle to eternal life too great to overcome. Because of him, our minds can be at peace. Our souls may rest.

I<small>N THE FALL OF</small> 1976 I gathered with about four or five hundred other teachers from the Church Educational System for an evening with Elder Bruce R. McConkie. We met in a chapel at the institute of religion adjacent to the University of Utah in Salt Lake City. Because of our admiration and respect for his gospel scholarship, as well as the meaningful occasions we had enjoyed with him before, we came to the meeting prepared to be filled. We were not disappointed. He spoke for about half an hour on the implications of the recent reorganization of the First Quorum of the Seventy. He spoke of priesthood, keys, and succession. At that point, without warning, he invited questions from the group. Some of the questions

CHAPTER 1

Who Will Be Saved?

tions related to our seminary course of study for the year, while others were about doctrinal matters in general. One question and the answer that followed changed my life; they affected the way I thereafter understood God, the plan of salvation, and how the gospel should be taught.

A young seminary teacher in the back of the chapel asked, in essence, "Elder McConkie, as you know, we are studying the New Testament in seminary this year. How do we keep our students from being discouraged (and how do we avoid discouragement

ourselves) when we read in the scriptures that strait is
the gate and narrow is the way that leads to life and few
there be that find it?" I will never forget the way the
answer came. Elder McConkie stood there at the pulpit
and said, "You tell your students that far more of our
Father's children will be exalted than we think!" The
chapel erupted in guarded but animated chatter among
the teachers. The seminary teacher came to his feet again
and followed up: "Could you please explain what you
mean?" "I'd be pleased to," Elder McConkie said.

BILLIONS OF SAVED BEINGS

What followed was one of the most enlightening
and eye-opening discussions I have ever experienced. In
thinking back, I suppose it lasted for twenty or thirty
minutes. After this many years, it is obviously impossible
to recall the exact words that were spoken, but I remember as if it were yesterday many of the important ideas
that Elder McConkie sought to convey, and, more particularly, what I felt. In substance and thought content,
and certainly in spirit, this is what was said:

Indeed, the scriptures speak often of a strait and
narrow path that leads to eternal life, and stress is frequently placed on the fact that few of the sons and
daughters of God will find their way to the end of that
path. But these are scriptural passages that must be
viewed in proper perspective. In the long run, we must

ever keep in mind that our Father and God is a suc-
cessful parent, one who will save many, many of his
children. Let us reason for a moment.

In comparison to the number of wicked souls
at any given time, perhaps the numbers of faithful followers seem small. But what of the children who have
died before the age of accountability—billions of little
ones from the days of Adam to the time of the Second
Coming, whom the scriptures affirm are "saved in the
celestial kingdom of heaven" (D&C 137:10)? What of
those through the ages who never had opportunity to
hear the message of the gospel in this life but who
(because of the yearnings in their heart for light and
truth) will receive it in the postmortal spirit world?

In the years since 1976 I have come across
prophetic support for this idea. In speaking of our
ancestors in the spirit world, President Wilford
Woodruff said at the April 1894 conference: "There will
be very few, if any, who will not accept the Gospel.
Jesus, while his body lay in the tomb, went and
preached to the spirits in prison, who were destroyed
in the days of Noah. After so long an imprisonment, in
torment, they doubtless gladly embraced the Gospel,
and if so they will be saved in the kingdom of God. The
fathers of this people will embrace the Gospel. . . . I tell
you when the prophets and apostles go to preach to
those who are shut up in prison, and who have not

received the Gospel, thousands of them will there embrace the Gospel. They know more in that world than they do here" (as cited in Boyd K. Packer, *The Holy Temple,* pp. 203, 206).

And, we might ask, what of the hosts of the righteous who qualified for exaltation from Enoch's city, Melchizedek's Salem, the golden era of the Nephites, or other holy societies of which we have no record? What of the countless billions of those children to be born during the glorious millennial era—during a time when disease and death and sin as we know it have neither sting nor victory over humankind? This will be that time of which the revelations speak, when "children shall grow up without sin unto salvation" (D&C 45:58). We agreed that it may well be that more persons will live on the earth during the thousand years of our Lord's reign—persons who are of at least a terrestrial nature—than the combined total of all who have lived during the previous six thousand years of the earth's temporal existence. Indeed, Elder McConkie asked us, who can count the number of saved beings in eternity? Our God, who is triumphant in all battles against the forces of evil, will surely be victorious in the numbers of his children who will be saved.

> OUR GOD WILL SURELY BE VICTORIOUS IN THE BATTLE TO SAVE MANY OF HIS CHILDREN.

CHARTING A COURSE OF RIGHTEOUSNESS

At the point where we as a congregation were riding a spiritual high, Elder McConkie popped our balloon momentarily with this comment: "But all of that doesn't have much to do with you and me, does it?" We sheepishly nodded in agreement and came back to earth. And then he explained that all faithful Latter-day Saints—those who chart their course toward eternal life, receive the ordinances of salvation, and strive with all their hearts to be true to their covenants—will gain eternal life. Even though they are certainly not perfect when they die, if they have sought to stay on course, in covenant, in harmony with the mind and will of God, they will be saved in the highest heaven. He said that we ought to have hope, that we needed to be positive and optimistic about attaining that glory. Then he startled us by saying, "I would suppose, for example, that I am now looking out upon a group of men and women who will all go to the celestial kingdom."

We left the chapel both electrified and sobered. I lay awake that night pondering what I had heard. I reflected on it again and again in the days and weeks that followed. Shortly thereafter, I sat down at the end of a very full and tiring Sabbath and turned on the television with the intention of watching a Brigham Young University devotional. To my surprise, the address was by Elder Bruce R. McConkie. It was a rebroadcast of a fireside he had delivered to the students, entitled "Jesus Christ and Him Crucified." After discussing the plan of salvation, the greatest truths and heresies in all eternity, and the vital role of Jesus Christ as Redeemer, Elder McConkie said: "As members of the Church, if we chart a course leading to eternal life; if we begin the processes of spiritual rebirth, and are going in the right direction; if we chart a course of sanctifying our souls, and degree by degree are going in that direction; and if we chart a course of becoming perfect, and, step by step and phase by phase, are perfecting our souls by overcoming the world, then it is absolutely guaranteed—there is no question whatever about it—we shall gain eternal life. Even though we have spiritual rebirth ahead of us, per-fection ahead of us, the full degree of sanctification ahead of us, if we chart a course and follow it to the best of our ability in this life, then when we go out of this life we'll continue in exactly that same course. We'll no longer be subject to the passions and the appetites of the flesh. We will have passed successfully the tests of this mortal probation and in due course we'll get the ful-ness of our Father's kingdom—and that means eternal life in his everlasting presence" ("Jesus Christ and Him Crucified," *1976 Devotional Speeches of the Year,* pp. 400–401).

Again I was touched and found myself ponder-ing the implications of these things for my own life, as well as that of my wife and family, and I wondered how I should change my approach to teaching the gospel.

When the October 1976 general conference came, Elder McConkie spoke on death, life beyond the grave, and the need for us to endure faithfully to the end. Among other things, he said: "All the faithful Saints, all of those who have endured to the end, depart this life with the absolute guarantee of eternal life.

"There is no equivocation, no doubt, no uncertainty in our minds. Those who have been true and faithful in this life will not fall by the wayside in the life to come. If they keep their covenants here and now and depart this life firm and true in the testimony of our blessed Lord, they shall come forth with an inheritance of eternal life.

"We do not mean to say that those who die in the Lord, and who are true and faithful in this life, must be perfect in all things when they go into the next sphere of existence. There was only one perfect man— the Lord Jesus whose Father was God. . . .

"But what we are saying is that when the saints of God chart a course of righteousness, when they gain sure testimonies of the truth and divinity of the Lord's work, when they keep the commandments, when they overcome the world, when they put first in their lives the things of God's kingdom: when they do all these things, and then depart this life—though they have not yet become perfect—they shall nonetheless gain eternal life in our Father's kingdom; and eventually they shall be perfect as God their Father and Christ His Son are perfect" (in *Conference Report,* October 1976, pp. 158–59).

Less than four years later, Elder McConkie delivered an address at Brigham Young University in which he identified as one of the "seven deadly heresies" the idea that we must be perfect in order to be saved. "If we keep two principles in mind," he observed, "we will thereby know that good and faithful members of the Church will be saved even though they are far from perfect in this life. These two principles are (1) that this life is the appointed time for men to prepare to meet God—this life is the day of our probation; and (2) that the same spirit which possesses our bodies at the time we go out of this mortal life shall have power to possess our bodies in that eternal world.

SATAN STRIVES TO DISCOURAGE US WHENEVER WE FALL SHORT. WE MUST NOT LET HIM.

"What we are doing as members of the Church is charting a course leading to eternal life. There was only one perfect being, the Lord Jesus. If men had to be perfect and live all of the law strictly, wholly, and completely, there would be only one saved person in eternity. The prophet [Joseph Smith] taught that there are many things to be done, even beyond the grave, in working out our salvation.

"And so what we do in this life is chart a course leading to eternal life. That course begins here and now and continues in the realms ahead. We must determine in our hearts and in our souls, with all the power and ability we have, that from this time forward we will press on in righteousness; by so doing we can go where God and Christ are. If we make that firm determination, and are in the course of our duty when this life is over, we will continue in that course in eternity" ("The Seven Deadly Heresies," *1980 Devotional Speeches of the Year,* pp. 78–79).

I have taken the time to quote rather extensively from one General Authority of the Church for two reasons. First, it is worthwhile to note the consistency in Elder McConkie's plea and invitation for us to have hope, to hold on, and to approach our challenges and vicissitudes optimistically. Second, I focused on Elder McConkie because of who he is. Latter-day Saints who are at least distantly acquainted with his sermons and writings, who know him as one of the significant doctrinal voices of this dispensation, also know him to be one who is firm, steadfast, and straightforward in his declaration of the plan of salvation and of what it takes for men and women to be saved. Few of us would be prone to accuse him of being too loose, too lax, too liberal on the divinely established standards for peace and joy here and for exaltation in eternity.

VISIONS OF THE MULTITUDES OF THE SAVED

There is no ceiling on the number of saved beings in eternity, no cap, no quota by which the Father of us all must and will be governed. Like any parent, he surely desires that all of his sons and daughters receive the message of salvation, work righteousness, and return to him honorably. Not all will, it is true. But many will—a great many.

Father Lehi, as a part of his dream/vision, beheld men and women from all walks of life (see 1 Nephi 8). In what might well be called the Parable of the Paths, Lehi saw how people, four groups of people, respond to truth and to what degree they are attracted to the good and the holy. This Parable of the Paths, like the Parable of the Soils in Matthew 13, is a study of spiritual receptivity. Lehi saw one group who obtained passage on the strait and narrow path but who, because of the mists of darkness or temptations of the devil, wandered off the path and were lost. A second group pressed forward to the end of the path and partook of the fruit. They were then lured away from further participation in gospel living because of embarrassment, which resulted from the taunting and ridicule of the worldly wise in a large and spacious building. A third group never made it to the path but instead blindly felt their way toward the large and spacious building.

Finally, Lehi "saw other multitudes pressing forward; and they came and caught hold of the end of the rod of iron; and they did press their way forward, continually holding fast to the rod of iron, until they came forth and fell down and partook of the fruit of the tree" (1 Nephi 8:30). And what became of them? We suppose they stayed faithful and endured to the end. They were saved. And how many were there? *Multitudes.*

In a similar way President Joseph F. Smith, who was blessed to behold in vision the postmortal spirit world only six weeks before his own death and entrance therein, remarked: "As I pondered over these things which are written"—the epistles of Peter—"the eyes of my understanding were opened, and the Spirit of the Lord rested upon me, and I saw the hosts of the dead, both small and great. And there were gathered together in one place"—we know it as paradise—"*an innumerable company of the spirits of the just, who had been faithful in the testimony of Jesus while they lived in mortality.* . . . All these had departed the mortal life, firm in the hope of a glorious resurrection, through the grace of God the Father and his Only Begotten Son, Jesus Christ" (D&C 138:11–14; emphasis added).

John the Revelator also had a vision of saved beings when he saw into heaven—meaning the celestial kingdom—"and I beheld, and I heard the voice of many angels round about the throne . . . and the number of them was ten thousand times ten thousand, and thousands of thousands" (Revelation 5:11). John saw 100 million angels surrounding the throne of God, plus "thousands of thousands" of others. What a multitude there are in the celestial kingdom!

It has been my privilege to associate with good men and women most of my life, men and women of faith and character, men and women who have received the gospel of Jesus Christ and are striving to abide by its precepts. They are people who are earnestly seeking to please the Lord, to serve the sheep of his fold, and to make a difference for good in a world that is in desperate need of goodness. They are people of covenant, people who have come out of the world and yearn to put off the natural man and come unto Christ. But they are not perfect. They make mistakes, feel regret, and often wonder about their standing before God.

> I HAVE A WITNESS, BURNED INTO MY SOUL AS THOUGH BY FIRE, THAT GOD IS MINDFUL OF EACH OF US.

Satan works tirelessly to lead us into major transgression. But he also strives to discourage us whenever we fall short of the standards we and God have set for ourselves. We simply must not let Satan discourage us.

I have a witness, burned into my soul as though by fire, that God is mindful of his children, that he has established a divine plan for the ultimate transformation of individuals and society. I also know that we can make it, make it to the celestial kingdom, if we stay on the gospel path, trust in and rely upon him who is mighty to save, press on, and never, ever give up.

It is often the case that the scriptures may be understood on many levels. Words and phrases and doctrinal concepts may mean a number of things, depending on the context, the audience, and the need at the time. For this reason, it is seldom wise to be overly zealous about exclusive definitions, singular interpretations, and formulas when it comes to comprehending holy writ. This principle is illustrated in Moroni's recitation to Joseph Smith of Malachi's prophecy concerning the coming of Elijah. In the midst of quoting numerous passages from the Old and New Testaments, Moroni quoted Malachi 4:5–6 quite differently from how it appears in the King James version. Did this new rendition invalidate the old one? Are the

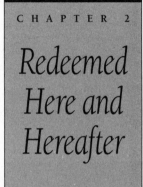

CHAPTER 2

Redeemed Here and Hereafter

renderings in our present Bibles inaccurate, or does Moroni's account simply represent another dimension of the prophecy? Knowing full well what Moroni had said in 1823, in 1842 the Prophet Joseph wrote an epistle to the Church in which he quoted the Malachi passage directly from the King James version. "I might have rendered a plainer translation to this," he said, "but it is sufficiently plain to suit my purpose as it stands" (D&C 128:18).

I have begun to notice in myself that when my study of the scriptures becomes wholly an intellectual endeavor, when it becomes more definitional than devotional, I have taken a detour. Twenty years ago I heard a noted Latter-day Saint scholar present a special lecture on a rather complex doctrinal matter. In the question-and-answer portion of the meeting a woman said, "Brother Jones, several times in your talk you used the word *sanctify.* Do you mean by that *purify?*" His response was rather unsettling to me: "Oh no, we must never confuse those two words. They are referring to two separate and distinct processes!" I shook my head in disbelief and wondered what possible good could come from drawing a distinction without a difference. Since then I have thought a good deal about doctrinal definitions. There is certainly some value to be derived from knowing what a concept means, but we must be careful not to limit the Lord or his prophets to one way of speaking or one avenue of meaning.

BECOMING PURE IN HEART

An illustration may be helpful. It seems to me that one of the most significant things we can do in this life is to become pure in heart. We are sent to earth to gain a body, to have experiences, and to learn to overcome the flesh and submit to the will of the Spirit. We are here to become good, to become noble, to become Christlike. We come into the true Church, receive the ordinances of salvation, enter the temple and establish eternal family units, and strive to serve one another and overcome the world—all in an effort to become Christlike, to become pure in heart, to qualify one day to be with God and to be like God. I don't completely understand how it is that a heart can begin to be softened and turned to the things of the Spirit, how it is exactly that our sins are remitted and filth and dross are burned out of our souls as though by fire. I know that it is done by virtue of the blood of Christ and through the medium of the Holy Ghost, but the particulars, the means, the specifics are not always clear to me. But God is merciful, and he wants us to grasp and appreciate to some degree what is taking place within us. And so he speaks through his servants, the prophets. He makes known many sacred things through these chosen messengers, including the process of human regeneration. They may approach a given doctrine from different perspectives, but they all teach the same message.

One prophet-leader says, in essence: "To me, having my sins remitted and becoming pure in heart is like being *born again.* It is like rising from spiritual death to life." Another prophet responds: "Yes, that certainly is true, but I see the process as much more practical, much more fundamental. Becoming pure in heart is being *converted,* being turned wholly to the ways and works of the Lord." A third Church leader adds his testimony: "I suppose I bring more of my legal background to this discussion than the others of you, but for me becoming pure in heart is being *justified*— exonerated, pronounced innocent, declared clean." A fourth covenant spokesman adds, "I like all that has been said, but my own experience testifies that becoming pure in heart is like a *baptism by fire.*"

> WHEN MY SCRIPTURE STUDY BECOMES AN INTELLECTUAL ENDEAVOR, I HAVE TAKEN A DETOUR.

The question is, which of the prophetic voices best describes becoming pure in heart? Is it a rebirth, a conversion, justification, or baptism by fire? The obvious answer is, yes—it is all of them. Each of these perspectives adds something to our understanding, and each of them provides insight into that which is inexplicable to unillumined man.

BEING REDEEMED

In addition to what we have already said, it is worth noting that many words have both present and ultimate meaning. For example, let us consider the word *redeem.* We all know that the ultimate form of redemption is salvation or exaltation in the highest degree of the celestial kingdom. Abinadi taught that Christ has redeemed us in that he has "granted salvation unto his people" (Mosiah 15:18). At the same time, he stated that such redemption was conditional: "The Lord redeemeth none such that rebel against him and die in their sins;

. . . that have known the commandments of God, and would not keep them. . . . For salvation cometh to none such; for the Lord hath redeemed none such; yea, neither can the Lord redeem such" (Mosiah 15:26–27).

In another vein, all men and women are redeemed in the sense that the spirit and the body of every mortal shall be inseparably joined. We know that "through the redemption which is made for [us] is brought to pass the resurrection from the dead. And the spirit and the body are the soul of man. And the resurrection from the dead is the redemption of the soul. And the redemption of the soul is through him that quickeneth all things" (D&C 88:14–17).

Moroni testified that God had "created Adam, and by Adam came the fall of man. And because of the fall of man came Jesus Christ, even the Father and the Son; and because of Jesus Christ came the redemption of man. And because of the redemption of man, which came by Jesus Christ, they are brought back into the presence of the Lord." Now note Moroni's broad definition of redemption, one in which all men and women have part: "Yea, *this is wherein all men are redeemed, because the death of Christ bringeth to pass the resurrection, which bringeth to pass a redemption from an endless sleep,* from which sleep all men shall be awakened by the power of God when the trump shall sound; . . . and all shall stand before his bar, being redeemed and loosed

from this eternal band of death, which death is a temporal death" (Mormon 9:12–13; emphasis added—see also
Helaman 14:17). Further, the sons of perdition are "the
only ones who shall not be redeemed in the due time of
the Lord, after the sufferings of his wrath" (D&C 76:38),
meaning they are the only ones who shall be resurrected
but not redeemed unto a kingdom of glory.

But what of our being redeemed in this life?
Simply stated, forgiveness of sin entails redemption from
sin. Christ came to redeem us from sin by virtue of his
atoning blood, which blessing we obtain through the
medium of the Holy Spirit as we experience a mighty
change of heart and as we receive sacred ordinances (see
Mosiah 5:2, 7–8; Alma 5:21; 9:27). Just prior to his
death, father Lehi exulted: "The Lord hath redeemed
my soul from hell; I have beheld his glory, and I am
encircled about eternally in the arms of his love"
(2 Nephi 1:15). That is, Lehi had been forgiven of his
sins, had through the atonement put off the natural man
and put on Christ, and had come to know the supernal
and sanctifying power of divine love.

Christ came into the world, as Lehi explained to
Jacob, to "redeem the children of men from the fall. And
because that they are redeemed from the fall they have
become free forever, knowing good from evil" (2 Nephi
2:26). Because of the knowledge and faith of the brother
of Jared, he was redeemed from the Fall and brought

back into the presence of Jehovah (see Ether 3:13). After three days of darkness and anguish of soul, Alma the Younger declared, "I have repented of my sins, and have been redeemed of the Lord; behold I am born of the Spirit" (Mosiah 27:24). When men and women are born again, when they are changed from their carnal and fallen state to a state of righteousness, when they come alive and are quickened in regard to the spiritual realm—when they experience these things, they are redeemed of the Lord, here, in this life. That redemption reaches also to those who die without law (see Moroni 8:22).

On the other hand, Amulek observed: "And [Christ] shall come into the world to redeem his people; and he shall take upon him the transgressions of those who believe on his name; and these are they that shall have eternal life, and salvation cometh to none else. Therefore the wicked remain as though there had been no redemption made, except it be the loosing of the bands of death" (Alma 11:40–41). In a like manner, Mormon taught that where faith is insufficient among the people to call down the signs and wonders of heaven, "they are as though there had been no redemption made" (Moroni 7:38). Truly, "only unto him that has faith unto repentance is brought about the great and eternal plan of redemption" (Alma 34:16; see also 42:13). The Savior cannot redeem his people in their sins, only from them (see Alma 11:34–37; Helaman 5:9–10).

ENTERING THE REST OF THE LORD

Another expression with multiple meanings is *entering the rest of the Lord.* By reading Alma 13 in context—as a part of a larger sermon—we begin to see that the idea of entering the rest of the Lord is a central theme. The word *rest* is mentioned in each of the final four verses of the preceding chapter. It is mentioned five times in chapter 13. It would appear that Alma is trying to point out that it is through the atoning blood of Christ and by the power of the holy priesthood that individuals and congregations are prepared and made ready to enter the rest of God.

> I WAS SUDDENLY IMMERSED IN THE MOST COMFORTING INFLUENCE I HAD EVER KNOWN.

In its ultimate sense, a person enters the rest of God when he or she begins to dwell in his presence (see Alma 57:36; 60:13). (We will talk more about that meaning shortly.) But in the present, in the here and now, we enter God's rest when we gain a testimony of the gospel and are brought out of worldly confusion into the peace and security that comes only from God.

As a young missionary in the Eastern States Mission I learned something about being at peace and entering into the rest of the Lord. My companion and I had moved into a small town in New Jersey, only to find that the local Protestant ministers had prepared their parishioners for our coming. At almost every door we approached, we were met by a smiling face and the words, "Oh, you must be the Mormons. This is for you." They would then hand us an anti-Mormon tract. We saved the pamphlets, stacked them in the corner of the living room of our apartment, and soon had a rather substantial pile of material. Out of sheer curiosity we began to read the stuff during lunchtime. I can still recall the dark and empty feelings that filled my soul as we encountered question after question about selected doctrines and specific moments in the history of the Church. My senior companion was no different; he was as unsettled as I was.

For weeks we did our work, but our hearts weren't in it. We went through the motions but, without saying much to each other, sensed that we couldn't do this indefinitely. I broke the ice at lunch one afternoon with the rather brutal query, "Elder Dyreng, what if the Church isn't true?"

His response: "I don't know."

I followed up: "What if the Baptists are right?" (There was a strong contingent of Baptists in the area.)

He said, "I just don't know."

Third question: "What if the Catholics are right? What if they have had the authority all along?"

His response: "I've been wondering the same thing." Then, presumably in an effort to cheer me up, he asked, "Elder Millet, do you think we are doing anything wrong? I mean, even if we are not a part of the true church, are we hurting anyone?" I sheepishly replied that we were probably not doing anything destructive. "Then," he concluded, "maybe we should keep working."

I asked with much pain in my voice, "Is that supposed to make me feel better? If so, it doesn't." He indicated that under the present circumstances it was the best he could do.

I am ashamed to admit that prior to this time I had never prayed intently about my testimony. I was raised in the Church. Mom and Dad had a testimony, and I knew that they knew. That always seemed adequate. But now I was up against the wall of faith, and suddenly what they knew did not seem sufficient to settle my troubled heart. I prayed and I pleaded. I begged the Lord for light, for help, for anything! These vexations of the soul went on for about a month. I had actually concluded (though I had not confided it to my companion) that if relief were not forthcoming shortly, I would pack my bags and go home. It did not seem proper to be engaged seriously in a cause about which I could not bear testimony.

We came home for lunch a few days later, and

my companion set about the task of making the soup and preparing the peanut butter. I collapsed in a large chair in the living room, removed my shoes, and loosened my tie. As I began to reflect once more on my testimony problem, my heart ached. My feelings were close to the surface at this point, and I yearned for deliverance from my pain. For some reason I reached to a nearby lamp table and picked up a copy of the pamphlet *Joseph Smith Tells His Own Story*. I began reading the opening lines. I came to the Prophet's statement that he was born on 23 December 1805 in Sharon, Windsor County, Vermont, and I was suddenly and without warning immersed in the most comforting and soothing influence I had ever known. It seemed at the time as if I were being wrapped in a large blanket as I began to be filled with the warmth of the Holy Spirit from head to toe. I wept as the spirit of conversion encompassed me and as I came to know assuredly that what we were doing was right and true and good. I did not hear specific words, but the feelings on that occasion seemed to whisper, "Of course it's true. You know that now, and you've known it for a long time."

At the same time, I had another feeling, which is particularly pertinent to the discussion of this chapter. The feeling was that the answers to my doctrinal and historical concerns were beyond my present capacity to comprehend. In time, I felt, the answers would come, answers that would be as satisfying to the mind as they were soothing to the heart. The answers did come, in fact, within a matter of months, and I then marveled at how something so simple could have been so problematic before.

> WE NEED
> NOT WAIT
> UNTIL THE
> RESURRECTION
> TO ENJOY
> REDEMPTION
> IN CHRIST.

The Spirit touched my heart and told me things my mind did not yet understand. He helped me move into a position where I could proceed confidently with my work until my head caught up with my heart. Before this experience I was in agony, was not at peace, and was subject to the nagging and uncomfortable power of doubt and uncertainty. Afterwards, I was at peace, at rest, secure in the knowledge that my faith was well founded. Truly, the rest of God is "the spiritual rest and peace which are born from a settled conviction of the truth in the minds of [individuals]." To enter into God's rest here is to enter into "the knowledge and love of God, having faith in his purpose and in his plan, to such an extent that we know we are right, and that we are not hunting for something else, we are not disturbed by every wind of doctrine, or by the cunning and craftiness of men who lie in wait to deceive." The rest of the Lord that we gain in this life is thus "rest from doubt, from fear, from apprehension of danger, rest from the religious turmoil of the world"

(Joseph F. Smith, *Gospel Doctrine,* pp. 126, 58). God's rest is to know the peace of the Spirit, to enjoy the blessing of the Comforter. It is what Jesus promised to disciples when he said, "Come unto me, all ye that labour and are heavy laden, and I will give you rest" (Matthew 11:28).

There is a second meaning to this phrase. Spirits enter the rest of God when they enter paradise, the abode of the righteous in the postmortal spirit world at the time of death. Alma explained to Corianton, "Then shall it come to pass, that the spirits of those who are righteous are received into a state of paradise, *a state of rest, a state of peace,* where they shall rest from all their troubles and from all care, and sorrow" (Alma 40:12; emphasis added). Indeed, it is a place and a condition wherein men and women "expand in wisdom, where they have respite from all their troubles, and where care and sorrow do not annoy" (Joseph F. Smith, *Gospel Doctrine,* p. 448). "The Lord suffereth the righteous to be slain," Captain Moroni wrote to Pahoran, "that his justice and judgment may come upon the wicked; therefore ye need not suppose that the righteous are lost because they are slain; but behold, they do enter into the rest of the Lord their God" (Alma 60:13).

A third dimension of "the rest of the Lord" is that which follows the resurrection and judgment, as we enter the celestial kingdom and receive exaltation. It is interesting that Mormon, speaking to the members of the Church in his day, uses *rest* in at least two ways. "Wherefore," he said, "I would speak unto you that are of the church, that are the peaceable followers of Christ, and that have obtained a sufficient hope by which ye can enter into the rest of the Lord"—meaning here in mortality—"from this time henceforth until ye shall rest with him in heaven" (Moroni 7:3). Abiding in the rest of the Lord in this life is in anticipation of the ultimate rest and peace to be had in eternal glory.

There is yet another sense in which the word *rest* is used in scripture:

"And this greater priesthood administereth the gospel and holdeth the key of the mysteries of the kingdom, even the key of the knowledge of God.

"Therefore, in the ordinances thereof, the power of godliness is manifest.

"And without the ordinances thereof, and the authority of the priesthood, the power of godliness is not manifest unto men in the flesh;

"For without this [the power of godliness] no man can see the face of God, even the Father, and live.

"Now this Moses plainly taught to the children of Israel in the wilderness, and sought diligently to sanctify his people that they might behold the face of God;

"But they hardened their hearts and could not endure his presence; therefore, the Lord in his wrath, for his anger was kindled against them, swore that they should not enter into his rest while in the wilderness, *which rest is the fulness of his glory.*

"Therefore, he took Moses out of their midst, and the Holy Priesthood also" (D&C 84:19–25; emphasis added).

This is a significant scriptural statement. Alma's invitation for the people of Ammonihah to enter into the rest of the Lord is built upon the notion that ancient Israel provoked God and proved unworthy of this blessing (see Alma 12:36–37). Moses desired to make available the highest privilege of the priesthood to Israel— the privilege of seeing the face of God, of coming directly into the divine presence. Of the Israelites, Jehovah said, "I have sworn in my wrath, that they shall not enter into my presence, *into my rest,* in the days of their pilgrimage" (JST Exodus 34:2; emphasis added). Here the rest of the Lord is equated with being received into the personal presence of the Lord while the recipients are still mortal.

RECEIVING ETERNITY'S BLESSINGS
IN MORTALITY

As we will see in the remainder of this book, many scriptural terms that describe life hereafter also describe a dimension of life here. We need not wait until the resurrection to enjoy redemption in Christ; we may be redeemed here and now, in the present, through repentance, forgiveness, rebirth, and divine submission. We long for that glorious day when we will be received into the highest heaven, but we rejoice in the fact that the sacred and settling peace we know as the rest of God may be experienced during our days of probation.

Amulek meant what he said when he taught that this life is the time for men to prepare to meet God (see Alma 34:32). Redemption here prepares us for redemption hereafter. Rest and peace here are harbingers of the glory that is to be.

THE SCRIPTURES ARE CONSISTENT in their declaration that "no unclean thing can enter into [God's] kingdom" (3 Nephi 27:19). In theory, there are two ways by which men and women may inherit eternal life. The first is simply to live the law of God perfectly, to make no mistakes. To do so is to be *justified*—pronounced innocent, declared blameless—by works or by law. If we were to keep the commandments completely (including receiving the ordinances of salvation), never deviating from the strait and narrow path throughout our mortal lives, then we would qualify for the blessings of the obedient. Then, through the redemption wrought by the Son of God, including his power to raise us from the dead and bring us back into his presence for judgment, we would qualify to dwell in celestial glory.

CHAPTER 3

Approved of the Lord

And yet we are very much aware of the terrible truth that all are unclean as a result of sin (see Romans 3:23). All of us have broken at least one of the laws of God, and therefore we have disqualified ourselves for justification by law. Moral perfection may be a possibility, but it is certainly not a probability. Jesus alone trod that path. "Therefore," Paul observed, "by the deeds of the law"—meaning the law of Moses, as well as any law of God—"there shall no flesh be justified in his sight" (Romans 3:20; compare 2 Nephi 2:5).

The second way to be justified is *by faith;* it is for the sinner to be pronounced clean or innocent through trusting in and relying upon the merits of Him who was perfect, clean, and innocent (see Romans 10:4; 2 Nephi 2:6–7). Jesus owed no personal debt to justice; the Holy One thus claims of the Father "his rights of mercy which he hath upon the children of men" (Moroni 7:27). Because we are guilty of transgression, no amount of good deeds on our part, no nobility independent of divine intercession, could make up for the loss. Truly, "since man had fallen he could not merit anything of himself" (Alma 22:14).

Thus He who loved us first (see 1 John 4:10, 19) reaches out to the lost and fallen, to the disinherited, and proposes a marriage. The Infinite One joins with the finite, the Finished with the unfinished, the Whole with the partial, the Perfect with the imperfect. Through covenant with Christ and thus union with the Bridegroom, we place ourselves in a condition to become fully formed, whole, finished.

"THE GREAT EXCHANGE"

The means by which the Savior justifies us is wondrous indeed. It entails what might be called "the great exchange." It is certainly true that Jesus seeks through his atoning sacrifice and through the medium of the Holy Spirit to *change* us, to transform us from fallen and helpless mortals into "new creatures in Christ." But there is more. Jesus offers to *exchange* with us.

In his epistle to the Philippians, Paul speaks of his own eagerness to forsake the allurements of the world in order to obtain the riches of Christ. "I count all things but loss," he said, "for the excellency of the knowledge of Christ Jesus my Lord: for whom I have suffered the loss of all things, and do count them but dung, that I may win Christ"—and now note this important addition—"and *be found in him, not having mine own righteousness, which is of the law, but that which is through the faith of Christ, the righteousness which is of God by faith*" (Philippians 3:8–9; emphasis added).

Paul's point is vital: justification comes by faith, by trusting *in Christ's righteousness,* in his merits, mercy, and grace (see Romans 10:1–4; compare 2 Nephi 2:3; Helaman 14:13; D&C 45:3–5). Though our efforts to be righteous are necessary, they will forevermore be insufficient. Paul teaches a profound truth—that as we come unto Christ by the covenant of faith, our Lord's righteousness becomes our righteousness. He justifies us in the sense that he *imputes* (or credits) his goodness to our account and takes our sin. This is the great exchange.

To the Corinthians Paul explained that "God was in Christ, reconciling the world unto himself, not imputing their trespasses unto them. . . . For *he* [God the Father] *hath made him* [Christ the Son] *to be sin for us,* who knew no sin; *that we might be made the righteousness of God in him*" (2 Corinthians 5:19, 21; emphasis added). As Paul explained elsewhere, Christ "hath redeemed us from the curse of the law, being made a curse for us" (Galatians 3:13; compare Hebrews 2:9).

AS WE COME UNTO CHRIST BY THE COVENANT OF FAITH, OUR LORD'S RIGHTEOUSNESS BECOMES OURS.

One Protestant theologian, John MacArthur, has written: "Justification may be defined as an act of God whereby he imputes to a believing sinner the full and perfect righteousness of Christ, forgiving the sinner of all unrighteousness, declaring him or her perfectly righteous in God's sight, thus delivering the believer from all condemnation. . . . It is a forensic reality that takes place in the court of God" (*The Gospel According to Jesus,* p. 197).

MacArthur also explained: "Justification is a divine verdict of 'not guilty—fully righteous.' It is the reversal of God's attitude toward the sinner. Whereas He formerly condemned, He now vindicates. Although the sinner once lived under God's wrath, as a believer he or she is now under God's blessing. Justification is more than simple pardon; pardon alone would still leave the sinner without merit before God. So when God justifies He imputes divine righteousness to the sinner. . . .

Justification elevates the believer to a realm of full acceptance and divine privilege in Jesus Christ." The harsh reality is that "the law demands perfection. But the only way to obtain perfect righteousness is by imputation—that is, being justified by faith" (*Faith Works: The Gospel According to the Apostles,* pp. 89–90, 103).

Since "all have sinned, and come short of the glory of God" (Romans 3:23), we are "justified only by his grace through the redemption that is in Christ Jesus," or in other words, "justified by faith alone without the deeds of the law" (JST Romans 3:24, 28). The comforting message of the gospel is that Jesus the Messiah has, "according to his mercy," offered to save us, "by the washing of regeneration, and renewing of the Holy Ghost; which he shed on us abundantly . . . ; that being justified by his grace, we should be made heirs according to the hope of eternal life" (Titus 3:5–7).

Those who enter the gospel covenant and thereafter seek to do their duty and endure to the end the Lord holds "guiltless" (3 Nephi 27:16; compare D&C 4:2). It is not that they are guiltless in the sense of having never done wrong; rather, the Holy One removes the blame and imputes—accounts or decrees to the repentant sinner, the one who comes unto Christ by covenant—His righteousness. "For as by one man's disobedience"—the fall of Adam—"many were made

sinners, so by the obedience of one"—Jesus Christ—
"shall many be made righteous" (Romans 5:19).

JUSTIFICATION IN MORTALITY

In one sense—in the present, in the here and
now—we are justified as our sins are forgiven. Whenever
we repent or turn away from our evil ways (the Hebrew
connotation of repentance); whenever we repent or
change our thoughts, attitudes, and desires (the Greek
connotation of repentance), we are justified—pronounced clean and free from sin and the demands of
divine justice.

To be justified by God is to be made clean in
spite of one's inability to repay the Master, to be made
innocent in spite of one's lack of moral perfection. It is
to be acquitted from sin through one's faith in Christ,
faith which manifests itself in the works of righteousness
(see Romans 2:6–7, 13; Galatians 5:6; Titus 3:8, 14). The
Lord Jesus compensates for the chasm between man's
simple striving and God's immutable standards of perfection, between where a man really is and where he
must eventually be.

Justification is both a journey and a destination,
a process as well as a condition. Sidney Sperry thus spoke
of justification as not only a matter of "acquittal" from guilt
and sin but also of "being regarded as righteous in a future
divine judgment." "A comparison may be made," Brother

Sperry noted, "by reference to a man on an escalator. We anticipate that he will reach a given floor if he stays on the escalator. So a person will eventually be justified"— meaning fully entitled to enter the Lord's presence—"but may be regarded as being so now, if he retains a remission of sins (Mosiah 4:26) and continually shows his faith in God" (*Paul's Life and Letters,* p. 176).

Another way of saying this is that when we come unto Christ by covenant, the Lord Jesus justifies or exonerates us in the here and now; he treats us now as if we were fully qualified to inherit eternal life. In process of time and as we remain "in Christ," meaning in covenant, the Holy Ghost, the sanctifier, works and labors with our soul, ridding us of filth and dross, transforming our actions and our desires.

In short, for the present God justifies or ratifies our actions, and the way we know we are approved of God is that he sends forth his Spirit upon us. We enjoy the peaceful assurance that he is pleased with our offering (see D&C 59:23). In time, and after we have been proven and tried, we are justified in the sense that our lives, our covenants, and our ordinances receive the ratifying and certifying approval of heaven.

I have met Latter-day Saints all over the Church who are faithful, diligent, and God-fearing individuals. They work hard, they pray hard, and they serve tirelessly. They live in a constant state of repentance and improvement, and they hope that some day they will become the kind of stuff out of which a celestial kingdom will be made. Many of them, however, feel anxiety about their standing before God and wonder whether their course in life is pleasing to the heavens. And yet I notice that they seem to enjoy the gifts of the Spirit in their lives; they teach and speak by the power of the Holy Ghost; and they have sufficient faith to be healed when they are ill. I notice too that they tend to be kind, gentle, meek, and charitable. All of these things are evidence that they are on course, that they are in the line of their duty, that God is pleased. These people are walking in proper paths; at the end of the path is eternal reward. We are justified when we remain in covenant.

> THE LORD COMPENSATES FOR THE CHASM BETWEEN MAN'S SIMPLE STRIVING AND GOD'S STANDARDS.

I remember walking down the crowded streets of New York City as a young missionary. My companion was a warm and gentle giant of a man, one who had been raised on a farm in Idaho and knew the meaning of hard work. He was humble, teachable, and delightfully congenial. I felt at home and at peace with him. One day I asked him, "Elder Carter, do you suppose you will ever make it to the celestial kingdom?"

I was startled at how quickly he shot back at me with an answer. "You bet, I will," he said. "Where else is there?"

My first reaction was to suppose pride on his part, but I knew that such was not part of his sweet nature. I wondered if maybe he simply didn't sense the significance of my question, but I knew him well enough to realize that he was neither ignorant nor naive. The certitude in his answer bespoke a quiet confidence, one born of the Spirit, one that I could not comprehend at the time but that makes perfect sense to me now.

I sat with Elder Carter over twenty years later in his home in Idaho. A speaking assignment in the area had brought me into contact with him once again. He asked me and my daughter to come to his home for lunch and spend the afternoon with his family. It proved to be a most memorable four-hour block of time. Elder Carter had returned from his mission, returned to the farm, and returned to the hard work of keeping body and soul together. He had married a lovely young woman, raised a large family, and kept the same simple perspective about life—about God and his plan, about obedience and covenants and ordinances, and about making it to the celestial kingdom—that he had as a twenty-one-year-old. As he walked me and my daughter to the car at the end of an afternoon together, he said, "Bob, I'm so pleased with what you have been able to do with your life. I'm excited about the education you have been able to receive. I envy you."

At this point my emotions were close to the surface. I looked into his weather-beaten but gentle face, that Christian countenance, and said, "No, my friend, I envy you. You have something really special here. Believe me." As we drove away, I turned to Rebecca and commented, "Now there's a real son of God."

I don't know whether Elder Carter would have been able to discuss at length what it means to be justified by the Spirit, but the peace of heaven was in his home and in his heart. Theology may underlie his daily walk, but religion is his bread and butter. Others may debate in gospel doctrine class what it means to be sealed up to eternal life, but he has slowly and almost imperceptibly acquired the divine nature. He is possessed of the sacred confidence that derives from a life well lived—one, I am certain, that was not flawless but was lived faithfully. He has surely made mistakes along the way, but his trust and his reliance are on the Master. He knows that there is much room for improvement, but he holds tenaciously to the promises of the Lord. The Lord loves him, and it shows.

MAINTAINING A JUSTIFIED STATE

King Benjamin spoke of the need for *retaining* a remission of sins from day to day. That is, he encouraged his people (and us as readers) to labor to maintain our justified, sin-free condition.

"And again I say unto you as I have said before, that as ye have come to the knowledge of the glory of God, or if ye have known of his goodness and have tasted of his love, and have received a remission of your sins, which causeth such exceedingly great joy in your souls, even so *I would that ye should remember, and always retain in remembrance, the greatness of God, and your own nothingness, and his goodness and long-suffering towards you,* unworthy creatures, and *humble yourselves even in the depths of humility, calling on the name of the Lord daily,* and standing steadfastly in the faith of that which is to come, which was spoken by the mouth of the angel.

"And behold, I say unto you," Benjamin continued, "that if ye do this ye shall always rejoice, and be filled with the love of God, and always retain a remission of your sins; and ye shall grow in the knowledge of the glory of him that created you, or in the knowledge of that which is just and true" (Mosiah 4:11–12; emphasis added).

Humility, meaning acceptance of our own limitations and inabilities coupled with an absolute acceptance of the power of God and a willing submission to his will, is what will enable us to remain in a justified state, to retain a remission of sins from day to day.

Benjamin spoke of another requirement that helps to prepare the people of God to live in a state of justification: "And now, for the sake of these things which I have spoken unto you—that is, for the sake of retaining a remission of your sins from day to day, that ye may walk guiltless before God—*I would that ye should impart of your substance to the poor, every man according to that which he hath, such as feeding the hungry, clothing the naked, visiting the sick and administering to their relief, both spiritually and temporally,* according to their wants" (Mosiah 4:26; emphasis added—see also Alma 4:13–14).

> WITHIN OUR REACH IS THE CONFIDENCE THAT COMES FROM A LIFE WELL LIVED— NOT FLAWLESS, BUT FAITHFUL.

Though justification comes to us by the grace of our Lord and Savior Jesus Christ (see D&C 20:30), we indicate our willingness to abide in Christ, to remain in covenant with the Master, by doing the work of the Master, by extending ourselves in service to his sheep.

As we seek to save a sinner from the error of his or her ways, we hide a multitude of sins, namely our own (see James 5:20). As we are true to the Restoration and thus bear testimony to all the world of the sacred things revealed to the Latter-day Saints, we are forgiven of our sins (see D&C 84:61); as we embark in the service of the Lord and serve with all our heart, might, mind, and strength, we are justified and thereby stand blameless before God (see D&C 4:2). Truly, charity prevents a multitude of sins, in ourselves as well as in others (see JST 1 Peter 4:8).

The Prophet Joseph Smith thus declared that "to be justified before God we must love one another: we must overcome evil; we must visit the fatherless and the widow in their affliction, and we must keep ourselves unspotted from the world: for such virtues flow from the great fountain of pure religion, strengthening our faith by adding every good quality that adorns the children of the blessed Jesus" (*Teachings of the Prophet Joseph Smith,* p. 76; compare James 1:27).

SEALED BY THE HOLY SPIRIT OF PROMISE— IN MORTALITY

This principle of receiving blessings in mortality also holds for being sealed by the Holy Spirit of Promise. In one sense—in the present, in the here and now—a young couple can go into the temple to be married for eternity, and if they approach that sacred covenant and ordinance reverently and worthily, it could appropriately be said of them that their marriage has been sealed by the Holy Spirit of Promise.

That is, the Holy Spirit of Promise, meaning the Holy Spirit promised to the Saints, the Holy Ghost, was present to manifest his approval and to place a type of ratifying seal upon what took place. That seal is maintained and made sure as the couple remain faithful to their covenants and endure to the end through dedicated service, through trust in and reliance upon Jesus Christ. "An act that is justified by the Spirit is one that is sealed by the Holy Spirit of Promise, or in other words, ratified and approved by the Holy Ghost" (Bruce R. McConkie, *Mormon Doctrine*, p. 408; see also *Doctrinal New Testament Commentary*, 3:333–36).

Our revelations thus speak of the candidates for exaltation as those who "overcome by faith, and are sealed by the Holy Spirit of promise, which the Father sheds forth upon all those who are just and true" (D&C 76:53).

SANCTIFICATION IN MORTALITY

We are *sanctified* when the Holy Ghost cleanses and renews our souls. Whereas justification is a decreed change of *standing*, sanctification is a change of *state*. "Sanctification is the work of God," one theologian has written, "whereby he sets the believer apart from sin. Sanctification is a practical reality, not simply a legal declaration. Sanctification involves a change in the sinner's character, not just a new standing before God" (MacArthur, *The Gospel According to Jesus*, p. 198). Also: "Justification frees us from the *guilt* of sin, sanctification from the *pollution* of sin. . . . God not only frees us from sin's penalty (justification), but He frees us from sin's tyranny as well (sanctification)" (MacArthur, *Faith Works*, pp. 109, 121; emphasis in original).

Elder Orson Pratt wrote of this purifying process as follows: "Without the aid of the Holy Ghost, a person . . . would have but very little power to change his mind, at once, from its habituated course, and to walk in newness of life. Though his sins may have been cleansed away, yet so great is the force of habit, that he would, without being renewed by the Holy Ghost, be easily overcome, and contaminated again by sin. Hence, it is infinitely important that the affections and desires should be, in a measure, changed and renewed, so as to cause him to hate that which he before loved, and to love that which he before hated: to thus renew the mind of man is the work of the Holy Ghost" ("The Holy Spirit," in *Orson Pratt: Writings of an Apostle,* p. 57).

What is true in regard to being justified is equally true in regard to being sanctified. We may in this life be sanctified in regard to certain sinful enticements. We may come to abhor sin (see 2 Nephi 9:49; Jacob 2:5; Alma 13:12), shake at its appearance (see 2 Nephi 4:31), and even have no more disposition to do evil (see Mosiah 5:2). But sanctification is a process, one that goes on minute by minute, day by day, and year by year. Of a chain smoker who had after baptism lost all desire for tobacco, it could appropriately be said that he had been sanctified in regard to that particular temptation. Of the divorced woman who had been abused by her former husband, but who had through the intercession of divine powers had bitterness and vengeance burned out of her soul, it could rightly be said that she had been sanctified in regard to her feelings. Of the promiscuous man who had come unto Christ and forsaken his past life, and who after conversion was no longer driven by lust, it could be said that in that thing he had been sanctified.

WE CAN KNOW BY THE QUIET BUT CERTAIN WITNESS OF HIS SPIRIT THAT OUR LIVES ARE APPROVED OF GOD.

Sanctification comes in time to those who yield their hearts to God (see Helaman 3:35), to those whose minds are single to the glory of God (see D&C 88:67–68), to those who trust in and seek after the redeeming grace of Him who calls his people to holiness.

In one sense, we will never be completely freed from the pull and tug of sin in this life. "Will sin be perfectly destroyed?" President Brigham Young asked. "No, it will not, for it is not so designed in the economy of heaven. . . . Do not suppose that we shall ever in the flesh be free from temptations to sin. Some suppose that they can in the flesh be sanctified body and spirit and become so pure that they will never again feel the effects of the power of the adversary of truth. Were it possible for a person to attain to this degree of perfection in the flesh, he could not die neither remain in a world where sin predominates. . . . I think we shall more or less feel the effects of sin so long as we live, and finally have to pass the ordeals of death" (*Journal of Discourses* 10:173).

Through Christ we become new creatures of the Holy Ghost, but we are creatures who are called to live in a fallen world. That is, we are "redeemed but wrapped in grave clothes of unredeemed flesh. We are like Lazarus, who came forth from the grave still wrapped from head to foot in his burial garments" (MacArthur, *Faith Works,* p. 117).

Sanctification may be a condition, but it is also a process. "Those who go to the celestial kingdom of heaven," Elder Bruce R. McConkie explained to BYU students in 1976, "have to be sanctified, meaning that they become clean and pure and spotless. They've had evil and sin and iniquity burned out of their souls as though by fire. . . . It is a process. Nobody is sanctified in an instant, suddenly. But if we keep the commandments and press forward with steadfastness after baptism, then degree by degree and step by step we sanctify our souls until that glorious day when we're qualified to go where God and angels are" ("Jesus Christ and Him Crucified," *1976 Devotional Speeches of the Year,* p. 399).

Each of us longs for the day when we can stand before our Savior confidently and comfortably, worthy and prepared to be with him and go where he goes. But the assurance that we are on course need not be a distant realization; we can know by the quiet but certain witness of his Spirit that our lives are approved of God. We can be at peace.

I REMEMBER THE SUNDAY AFTERNOON I turned to my wife and made a very serious commitment. We had been married but a few months and were very happy. In a sincere moment I indicated that I had every intention of being perfect by the age of thirty. She smiled kindly and wished me well, and the matter was dropped. I really believed in what I was doing. I determined to read and study and pray and labor for the next several years, and then, after attaining the notable plateau, I would work to help others reach the same spiritual height.

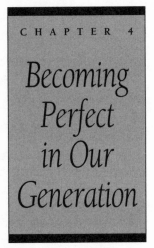

CHAPTER 4

Becoming Perfect in Our Generation

I suppose it isn't necessary to admit at this point that my goal was never quite achieved. Oh, I think I was a better man at thirty than I was at twenty-three, but I certainly wasn't perfect. Now almost twenty years after passing my initial goal, I still am not perfect in the sense I had originally intended to be, but I think I understand the process a little better now.

I supposed, in my naivete, if I just held my tongue, squelched my bitter feelings, blocked my thoughts, gritted my teeth, pushed myself to do my duty, and gripped the rod of iron white-knuckled-like for a sufficient time, that eventually such things would become quite natural and second nature to me. And I admit that many of what were once quite labored actions are now a bit more spontaneous. Over the years, however, I came to know that perfection in this life is not only difficult but impossible, at least as we usually define perfection.

It is one thing to attend all my church meetings, pay a full tithing and generous offerings, live the Word of Wisdom, and visit my home teaching families regularly. In a sense, I suppose, we can keep these laws perfectly if we simply do them and do them for the right reason. But at what point in my progression will I be able through sheer willpower to love my neighbor perfectly, evidencing in my attitudes and my actions such fruits of the Spirit as patience, long-suffering, gentleness, meekness, kindness, and the pure love of Christ? Where along the road to perfection will I no longer take offense, blame others, or harbor bitterness? One need not ponder on these matters for a lifetime before it becomes clear that becoming Christlike is a continuing pursuit that we simply cannot accomplish on our own.

Jesus' call to a higher righteousness, as embodied in the Sermon on the Mount, contained the penetrating and poignant statute: "Ye are therefore commanded to be perfect, even as your Father which is in heaven is perfect" (JST Matthew 5:50). Many months later that same Lord, now resurrected and glorified, commanded his Saints in the western hemisphere, "Therefore I would that ye should be perfect even as I, or your

Father who is in heaven is perfect" (3 Nephi 12:48). The directive has been given, the standard set. Nothing short of the ideal can possibly suffice: a being of absolute perfection could ask nothing less of his people.

PERFECTION IN THIS LIFE

"*Finite perfection,*" Elder Bruce R. McConkie has written, "may be gained by the righteous saints in this life. It consists in living a God-fearing life of devotion to the truth, of walking in complete submission to the will of the Lord, and of putting first in one's life the things of the kingdom of God" (*Mormon Doctrine,* p. 567; emphasis in original).

Only Jesus of Nazareth maintained a perfect walk in this life in the sense that he navigated the strait and narrow path without moral detour or transgression; he alone achieved moral perfection and completed mortality without flaw or error. But others have achieved perfection in the sense that they sought to do all that was commanded them, in the sense that they gave themselves wholly to the accomplishment of the will of the Lord. The scriptural record attests that "Noah found grace in the eyes of the Lord; for Noah was a just man, and *perfect in his generation;* and he walked with God, as did also his three sons, Shem, Ham, and Japheth" (Moses 8:27; emphasis added—compare Genesis 6:9). The same is said of Seth, the son of Adam (see D&C

107:43). Further, "there was a man in the land of Uz, whose name was Job; and *that man was perfect and upright,* and one that feared God, and eschewed evil" (Job 1:1; emphasis added).

What do the scriptures mean when they speak of a person being "perfect in his generation"? President Brigham Young declared that "we all occupy diversified stations in the world, and in the kingdom of God. Those who do right, and seek the glory of the Father in heaven, whether their knowledge be little or much, or whether they can do little or much, if they do the very best they know how, they are perfect. . . .

> BECOMING CHRISTLIKE IS A CONTINUING PURSUIT THAT WE CANNOT ACCOMPLISH ON OUR OWN.

"'Be ye as perfect as ye can,' for that is all we can do tho' it is written, 'Be ye perfect as your Father who is in heaven is perfect.' To be as perfect as we possibly can according to our knowledge, is to be just as perfect as our Father in heaven is. He cannot be any more perfect than he knows how, any more than we. When we are doing as well as we know how, in the sphere, and station which we occupy here, we are justified. . . . We are as justified as the angels who are before the throne of God" (*Journal of Discourses* 2:129–30).

Other than the Lord Jesus, who is the prototype of all perfect and saved beings, the standard of perfection against which we measure our own lives is within us. Though we may admire the lives of the apostles and prophets, though we may be deeply impressed by the examples of those who appear to do so well what they are called to do, we are seldom benefited by comparing ourselves with others. Comparisons of this sort are usually misleading and inappropriate, for we who so often see only the exterior (and thus what *appears* to be) cannot know of the inner trials, the hidden battles of the soul, the less visible crosses that are borne. And so it is that we are called upon to do our best in the circumstances in which we may be placed. Just as members of the Church are never assigned to magnify another person's calling, so we are not expected to measure ourselves against another's life.

In highlighting some of the challenges we face in this modern world, Elder Boyd K. Packer spoke of the "moral pollution" all about us. "It is a great challenge," he stressed, "to raise a family in the darkening mists of our moral environment. We emphasize that the greatest work you will do will be within the walls of your own home (see Harold B. Lee, in *Conference Report,* April 1973, p. 130; or *Ensign,* July 1973, p. 98), and that 'no other success can compensate for failure in the home' (see David O. McKay, in *Conference Report,* April 1935, p. 116; quoting J. E. McCulloch, *Home: The*

Savior of Civilization [Washington, D.C.: The Southern Co-operative League, 1924], p. 42).

"The measure of our success as parents, however, will not rest solely on how our children turn out. That judgment would be just only if we could raise our families in a perfectly moral environment, and that now is not possible.

"It is not uncommon for responsible parents to lose one of their children, for a time, to influences over which they have no control. They agonize over rebellious sons and daughters. They are puzzled over why they are so helpless when they have tried so hard to do what they should." And then comes this marvelous ray of hope: "It is my conviction that those wicked influences one day will be overruled" (in *Conference Report,* April 1992, p. 94).

These comforting remarks not only provide hope for families torn asunder by the pulls of the world, but they also set forth an important principle—that the God of heaven only expects us to do the best we can in our given circumstances. When we have made an offering that is acceptable (and he can and will let us know when it is acceptable), then we must be willing to step back, let go, and let God; we must be willing to cast our burdens on him and trust in his eternal wisdom and omnipotence. There is consummate comfort to be had in this form of surrender.

A careful search of holy writ affirms that there

are certain activities, certain labors, certain blessings
from God that move men and women toward finite perfection in this life and on toward that perfection that
prevails among the gods hereafter. Paul explained that
the Church of Jesus Christ—the organization, offices,
councils, and ordinances—had been established "for
the perfecting of the saints, for the work of the ministry,
for the edifying of the body of Christ" (Ephesians 4:12;
see also JST Hebrews 6:1–2). Paul wrote to Timothy
that "all Scripture given by inspiration of God, is profitable for doctrine, for reproof, for correction, for
instruction in righteousness: that the man of God may
be perfect, throughly furnished unto all good works"
(JST 2 Timothy 3:16–17). Paul also taught that those
who have gone before us—who were denied access to
the gospel covenant because it was unavailable to
them—cannot be made perfect without us, without our
vicarious assistance; neither can we be made perfect
without the appropriate ties between ancestry and pos-
terity, between roots and branches (see Hebrews 11:40;
D&C 128:15). In addition, the prophets have taught
that patience (see James 1:4) and suffering (see Hebrews
2:10; 5:8; 1 Peter 5:10) mold men and women toward
that perfection that allows them to feel confidence in
the presence of Him who is the embodiment of whole-
ness and completion.

God has provided through the Holy Ghost the

precious gifts and fruit of the Spirit that help to move us along the strait and narrow path toward perfection. As the Revelator, the Holy Ghost helps us to know and feel heavenly things and in time to gain "the mind of Christ" (1 Corinthians 2:16), to think as he thinks, feel as he feels, act as he would act. The Prophet Joseph Smith taught: "A person may profit by noticing the first intimation of the spirit of revelation; for instance, when you feel pure intelligence flowing into you, it may give you sudden strokes of ideas, so that by noticing it, you may find it fulfilled the same day or soon; i.e., those things that were presented unto your minds by the Spirit of God, will come to pass; and *thus by learning the Spirit of God and understanding it, you may grow unto the principle of revelation, until you become perfect in Christ Jesus*" (*Teachings of the Prophet Joseph Smith,* p. 151; emphasis added).

> WE CAN BE PERFECT IN THE SENSE THAT WE DO OUR BEST, THEN RELY WHOLLY UPON THE MERCY OF CHRIST.

In process of time, the Sanctifier purges and purifies the human heart, welds our souls to principles and practices of godliness, and prepares us for association with holy beings. Mormon therefore taught that charity, the pure love of Christ, is bestowed upon the true followers of Jesus Christ, not only to motivate them to serve others (as important as that is), but also that they "may become the sons of God; *that when he shall appear we shall be like him,* for we shall see him as he is; that we may have this hope; that we may be purified even as he is pure" (Moroni 7:48; emphasis added).

The gifts and fruit of the Spirit "are given by Him for the perfection of His people," President George Q. Cannon observed, "that in this vale of tears, shut out as we are from his presence, a veil of darkness having been drawn, as it were, between us and Him, those who will exercise faith in His promises and will keep His commandments may receive the aid that is necessary to enable them to walk before Him and to enjoy His power. . . .

"How many of you, my brethren and sisters, are seeking for these gifts that God has promised to bestow? How many of you, when you bow before your Heavenly Father in your family circle or in your secret places, contend for these gifts to be bestowed upon you? How many of you ask the Father, in the name of Jesus, to manifest Himself to you through these powers and these gifts? Or do you go along day by day like a door turning on its hinges, without having any feeling upon the subject, without exercising any faith whatever; content to be baptized and be members of the Church, and to rest there, thinking that your salvation is secure because you have done this?

"I say to you, in the name of the Lord, as one of His servants, that you have need to repent of this. You have need to repent of your hardness of heart, of your indifference, and of your carelessness. There is not that diligence, there is not that faith, there is not that seeking for the power of God that there should be among a people who have received the precious promises we have. . . .

"I say to you that it is our duty to avail ourselves of the privileges which God has placed within our reach. . . .

"I feel to bear testimony to you, my brethren and sisters, . . . that God is the same today as He was yesterday; that God is willing to bestow these gifts upon His children. . . . *If any of us are imperfect, it is our duty to pray for the gift that will make us perfect. Have I imperfections? I am full of them. What is my duty? To pray to God to give me the gifts that will correct these imperfections. If I am an angry man, it is my duty to pray for charity, which suffereth long and is kind. Am I an envious man? It is my duty to seek for charity, which envieth not. So with all the gifts of the Gospel.* They are intended for this purpose. No man ought to say, 'Oh, I cannot help this; it is my nature.' He is not justified in it, for the reason that God has promised to give strength to correct these things, and to give gifts that will eradicate them. If a man lack wisdom, it is his duty to ask God for wisdom. The same with everything else. That is the design of God concerning His Church. He wants His Saints to be perfected in the truth. For this purpose He gives these gifts, and bestows them upon those who seek after them, in order that they may be a perfect people upon the face of the earth, notwithstanding their many weaknesses, because God has promised to give the gifts that are necessary for their perfection" ("Discourse," *Millennial Star* 56 [1894]: 260–61; emphasis added—see also *Gospel Truth,* pp. 154–55).

BECOMING PERFECT IN CHRIST

"*Infinite perfection* is reserved for those who overcome all things and inherit the fulness of the Father in the mansions hereafter. It consists in gaining eternal life, the kind of life which God has in the highest heaven within the celestial world" (McConkie, *Mormon Doctrine,* p. 567; emphasis in original).

Though you and I cannot enjoy infinite perfection in the present, in the here and now, we can be perfect in the sense that we do the best we can and then rely wholly upon the merits and mercy of our Redeemer (see 2 Nephi 31:19; Moroni 6:4). That is, we can be "perfect in Christ" (Moroni 10:32). It is not that we must become sin-free in this life in order to be saved, though we ever press toward that glorious eventuality. Rather, it is expected that after we sin we return quickly to the light through godly sorrow and repentance.

In one sense, to be perfect is to be complete,

whole, mature, fully focused. We become perfect in Christ in the sense that we yield to the will of Christ, become one with him through the Holy Spirit, and become whole, fully formed, and complete. God declares us perfect in the here and now. If we remain in covenant, if we strive to be faithful to our promises throughout our lives, we will in time or eternity become fully perfect. In my colleague Stephen Robinson's words, "In the new covenant of faith, perfect innocence is still required, but it is required of the team or partnership of Christ-and-me, rather than of me alone. Because Christ and I are one in the gospel covenant, God accepts our combined total worthiness, and together Christ and I are perfectly worthy" (*Believing Christ,* p. 43). As it is with being justified, and as it is with being sanctified, perfection is both a process and a condition. But whether we speak of a person being "perfect in his generation" or of that ultimate perfection that comes hereafter, we speak of something that is brought to pass only through the intervention of God. Man cannot justify himself. He cannot sanctify himself. And he certainly cannot perfect himself. The transformations from a fallen nature to a spiritual nature, from worldliness to holiness, from corruption to incorruption, and from imperfection to perfection are

> AFTER WE SIN WE MUST RETURN QUICKLY TO THE LIGHT THROUGH GODLY SORROW.

accomplished because divine powers bring them to pass. They are acts of grace.

The Apostle Paul wrote to the early Christians: "Now *the God of peace,* that brought again from the dead our Lord Jesus, that great shepherd of the sheep, through the blood of the everlasting covenant, *make you perfect in every good work to do his will, working in you that which is wellpleasing in his sight,* through Jesus Christ; to whom be glory for ever and ever" (Hebrews 13:20–21; emphasis added).

The chief Apostle warned the Saints late in the first century: "Be sober, be vigilant; because your adversary the devil, as a roaring lion, walketh about, seeking whom he may devour: whom resist stedfast in the faith, knowing that the same afflictions are accomplished in your brethren that are in the world. But *the God of all grace,* who hath called us unto his eternal glory by Christ Jesus, after that ye have suffered a while, *make you perfect,* stablish, strengthen, settle you" (1 Peter 5:8–10; emphasis added). More specifically, people are made "perfect in Christ Jesus" (Colossians 1:28); they become "just men made perfect through Jesus the mediator of the new covenant, who wrought out this perfect atonement through the shedding of his own blood" (D&C 76:69). It would never be appropriate to lower the lofty standard held out to followers of Christ. Nor are our actions or attitudes approved of God if we suggest that the Savior did not mean what he said when he called us to the transcendent state of perfection. Our task is not to water down the ideal, nor to dilute the directive. Rather, we must view our challenge with perspective, from an eternal perspective, from the perspective provided by the unified message of all scripture.

"The command *Be ye perfect* is not idealistic gas," C. S. Lewis remarked. "Nor is it a command to do the impossible. He is going to make us into creatures that can obey that command. He said (in the Bible) that we were 'gods' and He is going to make good His words. If we let Him—for we can prevent Him, if we choose—He will make the feeblest and filthiest of us into a god or goddess, dazzling, radiant, immortal creature. . . . The process will be long and in parts very painful; but that is what we are in for. Nothing less. He meant what He said" (*Mere Christianity,* pp. 174–75).

LET ME RECONSTRUCT A SCENE that is rather familiar to most of us. We attempt to explain the message of the Restoration to a member of a Protestant church only to have them remark: "Thank you, but I'm a saved Christian." We recoil, turn off, or, I suppose in some cases, even try to argue with them about what they mean. Or we may respond as my father did so many times: "Yes, of course you are saved; you are saved from the grave." But that's obviously not what they intended.

CHAPTER 5

A Saved Mormon

In like fashion, when a Protestant asks us, "Are you a saved Christian?" we stumble over our words and wonder about how to respond. Generally, even if we do not voice our feelings, we want to stress that one is not saved until he or she endures to the end of their mortal life.

It is unfortunate that a topic like being saved carries with it so much emotional baggage (and thus so many barriers between us and others of our Father's children) that we are not in a position to communicate even our differences appropriately. Over the years as I have spoken openly with friends or colleagues from other faiths, I have come to appreciate a little better what they are saying. Some mean that they have received in their hearts a witness that Jesus is the Christ, that the Savior has forgiven their sins and they are now willing to turn their lives over to him, and that they are now in a saved condition in regard to happiness here and eternal reward hereafter. For them, to be converted to Christ is to be saved. It is to have what we might call the assurance of eternal life.

I have no reason to doubt their sincerity or the reality of their witness of Christ; the influence of the Holy Ghost is real, available, and the source of the testimony of Jesus. I know there are people out there who feel that once they profess Jesus with their lips they are saved forevermore and that what they do thereafter with their lives in terms of goodness and morality is immaterial. Yes, there are such people, but I don't know many of them. Most of the Protestants I grew up with—and most of the ministers and theologians I have encountered since—really do see a close tie between their saved condition and a righteous, God-fearing life. Those who are serious students of the New Testament understand the central message of the second chapter of James—that good works flow from the regenerate heart, that righteousness evidences true faith. Clearly, other Christian churches have much truth.

I know without any equivocation that there was an apostasy, a loss of plain and precious truths, a loss of priesthood authority. I know that God began the restoration of truths and powers through Joseph Smith and will

continue that restoration into and through the
Millennium. There's no question in my mind about any
of that.

But to say that the Baptists or the Methodists or
the Pentecostals do not possess the authority to act in
the name of God is not to say that they have no truth or
that any scriptural interpretation from them is automat-
ically incorrect or corrupt. Though the fulness of the
gospel is to be found only in The Church of Jesus Christ
of Latter-day Saints, remnants of truth, elements of
enlightenment, and aspects of the faith of the former-day
saints may be found throughout modern Christianity.

One example of this is the doctrine of "being
saved," which we generally consider to be a Protestant
idea. I would like to propose a sense in which Latter-
day Saint theology encompasses the notion of being
saved, here and now, in this life.

None of us has a problem speaking of a worthy
couple married in the temple as having been *sealed,* or
having had their union sealed by the Holy Spirit of
Promise. We know that the sealing is contingent or con-
ditioned upon faithful observance of their covenants,
but we do not hesitate to speak of John and Mary having been sealed in the temple.

And yet we are nervous as kittens about this
matter of being *saved.* It is not unlike a situation I found
myself in many years ago. Before leaving on a mission I

approached one of my priesthood leaders with the question, "What does it mean to be saved by grace?" Having been raised in the southern states and in the Bible Belt, I had heard the phrase many times from my Protestant friends.

> WHEN WE ARE HONEST WITH OURSELVES, WE KNOW THAT MOST OF OUR SINS ARE AGAINST CHARITY.

My priesthood leader—a powerful preacher of the gospel and one who knew the doctrines of the gospel quite well—responded quickly: "We don't believe in that."

I asked further: "We don't believe in salvation by grace? Why not?"

His comeback: "Because the Baptists do!" That response speaks volumes.

I don't expect that many of us will adopt the terminology of many modern Christians or of those who believe they were saved at the time they received Jesus into their hearts. Nor do I think we should. But it certainly wouldn't hurt us to better understand them.

ARE THERE SAVED MORMONS?

We know, in the words of Joseph Smith, that to be saved is to be placed beyond the power of all our enemies (see *Teachings of the Prophet Joseph Smith,* pp. 301, 305). He taught further that "salvation consists in the glory, authority, majesty, power and dominion which Jehovah possesses and in nothing else; and no being can possess it but himself or one like him." To be saved, then, is to be conformed into the image of Christ, to become like unto the prototype of all saved beings (*Lectures on Faith,* 7:9, 16).

Obviously salvation can also have a more limited dimension—meaning salvation from the grave, salvation from physical death. All mortals will be resurrected and thus enjoy this aspect of salvation. With but few exceptions, however, when the prophets speak of salvation they are referring to the highest of eternal rewards hereafter. (Examples of these exceptions include D&C 76:43–44, 88; 132:17; *Teachings of the Prophet Joseph Smith,* p. 12.) Salvation is redemption, exaltation, eternal life, and eternal lives; each of these terms means the same thing, but each lays stress on a particular aspect of the saved condition. And so, in the ultimate meaning, to be saved is to qualify for exaltation in the celestial kingdom—to be endowed with a fulness of the glory of the Father and to enjoy a continuation of the family unit into eternity (see D&C 132:19).

But now to the question: Do Latter-day Saints believe that men and women may enjoy the benefits of salvation only in the world to come? Is there no sense in which we may be saved in the present, in the here and now?

Though I quickly acknowledge that most

scriptural references to salvation seem to point toward that which comes in the next life, we do have within our theology principles and doctrines that suggest a form of salvation in this life. Perhaps the most obvious illustration is when a member of the Church makes his or her calling and election sure. As Joseph Smith taught, when we exercise saving faith and demonstrate our willingness to serve God at all hazards, we eventually, in this life or the next (see D&C 14:7; 50:5; 58:2), receive the assurance of eternal life (see *Teachings of the Prophet Joseph Smith,* pp. 149–50).

If the more sure word of prophecy, the knowledge that we are sealed up unto eternal life (see D&C 131:5), comes to us in this life, then our salvation is secure, or we might say, fairly secure. In fact, there is never a time in this life when faithful endurance to the end is not required. The scriptures teach that a man or woman may fall from grace and depart from the living God, that even the sanctified must take heed lest they fall (see D&C 20:30–34; 124:124), that those who were once enlightened and have tasted the heavenly gift may fall away (see Hebrews 6:4–6). Those who have been sealed to eternal life are no doubt fully aware of the fact that they must stay faithful to the end, yet they also know with full assurance that if they do so endure, they will be exalted, whether they die today or in a century.

Thus they are saved, or, to put it another way,

they are living in a saved condition. That may not be exactly what our Protestant brothers and sisters have in mind when they speak of being saved, but it's not far removed. Thus there is indeed a condition or state you and I may attain unto in this mortal life in which salvation hereafter is promised here; the day of judgment has essentially been advanced.

But is there any way to know we are saved other than receiving the more sure word of prophecy? I think there is. That same Holy Spirit of Promise that searches the hearts of men and women, that ratifies and approves and seals ordinances and lives, that same Holy Spirit serves, as Paul indicates, as the "earnest of our inheritance" (Ephesians 1:14).

Though this passage refers specifically to being sealed up unto eternal life, I believe the principle is also true in regard to our qualifying for and cultivating the gift and influence of the Holy Ghost. That is, the Lord sends to us "the earnest of the Spirit" (2 Corinthians 1:21–22; 5:5) as an evidence that our lives are in order. The Lord's "earnest money" on us, his down payment, his indication to us that he will save us, is the Holy Spirit. We know that we are on course when we have the companionship of the Spirit. We know that our lives are approved of God when we have the companionship of the Spirit. We know that we are in Christ, in covenant, when we have the companionship of the

Spirit. And we know, I suggest, that we are saved when we truly have the constant companionship of the Spirit.

If we live in such a way that we can take the sacrament worthily, hold and utilize a current temple recommend, maintain the gift and gifts of the Spirit (including the greatest gifts of faith, hope, and charity), and in all things yield our hearts to God (see Helaman 3:35; D&C 20:31), then we are in the line of our duty; we are approved of the heavens, and if we were to die suddenly, we would go into paradise and eventually into the celestial kingdom.

> WE ARE LIVING IN A SAVED CONDITION TO THE EXTENT THAT WE ARE LIVING IN THE LIGHT.

REPENTANCE TO STAY IN THE PATH

The King James Version of 1 John 3:9 states: "Whosoever is born of God doth not commit sin." The problem is, as you know and I know, that those who have been born again are not free from sin. But they repent quickly (see D&C 109:21). They move rapidly from the darkness back into the light. They live always in a spirit of repentance.

President Brigham Young gave this important explanation regarding living in a constant state of worthiness: "I do not recollect that I have seen five minutes since I was baptized that I have not been ready to preach a funeral sermon, lay hands on the sick, or to pray in private or in public. I will tell you the secret of this. In all your business transactions, words, and communications, *if you commit an overt act, repent of that immediately, and call upon God to deliver you from evil and give you the light of His Spirit. . . . If I commit an overt act, the Lord knows the integrity of my heart, and, through sincere repentance, He forgives me"* (*Journal of Discourses* 12:103; emphasis added).

I had an experience that helps to illustrate the idea of "immediate repentance." I had come home from work after a very long day, a day in which everything that could have gone wrong had gone wrong (or so it seemed). I was physically exhausted and emotionally spent. I sat in my recliner and had begun to doze off when my wife Shauna came into the room; her mood seemed much too happy for what I had experienced in the previous twelve hours. "How was your day, honey?" she asked. Without catching myself, I sat up in my chair and sarcastically responded that she wouldn't understand if I took the time to explain. I immediately saw the pain in her eyes as she quickly made her way to another part of the house.

I was disgusted with myself. I sensed that she had been trying to be nurturing and loving, to lift my spirits. I grieved over my indiscretion against charity and found myself thinking: "Oh, no! Now it will take me three days to get the Spirit of the Lord back." In less than one minute I found myself responding to the first feeling: "Oh, no, it won't! I'm going deal with this right now."

I hopped out of the chair, went into the bedroom, and said to her: "It's been a miserable day. The walls have been crashing down all day long. But that's no reason to react meanly to you. I'm sorry. Will you forgive me?" She readily nodded and hugged me. I went back to my chair, silently asked the Lord to forgive me, and immediately felt the peace of the Spirit return. I was back in the light.

Obviously, more serious sins require more time, deeper repentance, and a period of appropriate godly sorrow. But when we are honest, truly honest with ourselves and with the Lord, we quickly acknowledge that most of our sins are inadvertent sins against charity.

"When men truly and heartily repent," President Young taught, "and make manifest to the heavens that their repentance is genuine by obedience to the requirements made known to them through the laws of the Gospel, then are they entitled to the administration of salvation, and no power can withhold the good Spirit from them" (*Journal of Discourses* 10:18).

The Joseph Smith Translation of 1 John 3:9 reads as follows: "Whosoever is born of God *doth not continue in sin;* for the Spirit of God remaineth in him; and he cannot continue in sin, because he is born of God, *having received that holy Spirit of promise*" (emphasis added).

If we have the Holy Spirit, he will bring with him a spirit of peace. A modern revelation attests: "But learn that he who doeth the works of righteousness shall receive his reward, even peace in this world, and eternal life in the world to come" (D&C 59:23). Indeed, we might liken to ourselves the words the Lord said to Oliver Cowdery: "If you desire a further witness, cast your mind upon the night that you cried unto me in your heart, that you might know concerning the truth of these things. *Did I not speak peace to your mind . . . ? What greater witness can you have than from God?*" (D&C 6:22–23; emphasis added).

THE PROMISE OF PRESENT SALVATION

We've talked about the presence of the Spirit in our lives being an indicator of our status before God. There is another measurement I would suggest. I believe that we are living in a saved condition to the extent that we are living in the light, living according to our spiritual privileges, and living in harmony with the knowledge and the blessings we have received to that point in our lives. The following is an intriguing statement from President Brigham Young:

"If a person with an honest heart, a broken, contrite, and pure spirit, in all fervency and honesty of soul, presents himself and says that he wishes to be baptized for the remission of his sins, and the ordinance is administered by one having authority, is that man saved? Yes, to that period of time. Should the Lord see proper to take him then from the earth, the man has believed and been baptized, and is a fit subject for heaven—a candidate for the kingdom of God in the celestial world, because he has repented and done all that was required of him to that hour. . . .

> HE WILL EXTEND TO US THAT MARVELOUS ENABLING POWER SO ESSENTIAL TO DAILY LIVING.

"*It is present salvation and the present influence of the Holy Ghost that we need every day to keep us on saving ground.* When an individual refuses to comply with the further requirements of Heaven, then the sins he had formerly committed return upon his head; his former righteousness departs from him, and is not accounted to him for righteousness: but if he had continued in righteousness and obedience to the requirements of heaven, *he is saved all the time, through baptism, the laying on of hands, and obeying the commandments of the Lord* and all that is required of him by the heavens—the living oracles. He is saved now, next week, next year, and continually, and is prepared for the celestial kingdom of God whenever the time comes for him to inherit it.

"*I want present salvation.* I preach, comparatively, but little about the eternities and Gods, and their wonderful works in eternity; and do not tell who first made them, nor how they were made; for I know nothing about that. *Life is for us, and it for us to receive it today, and not wait for the Millennium.* Let us take a course to be saved today, and, when evening comes, review the acts of the day, repent of our sins, if we have any to repent of, and say our prayers; then we can lie down and sleep in peace until the morning, arise with gratitude to God, commence the labors of another day, and strive to live the whole day to God and nobody else" (*Journal of Discourses* 8:124–25; emphasis added).

I am concerned that far too many Latter-day Saints wrestle with feelings of inadequacy, struggle with hopelessness, and in general are much too anxious about their standing before God. It is important to keep the ultimate goal of exaltation in our minds, but it seems so much more profitable to focus on fundamentals and on the here and now—staying in covenant, being true to our promises, cultivating the gift of the Holy Ghost.

"I am in the hands of the Lord," President Young pointed out, "and never trouble myself about my salvation, or what the Lord will do with me hereafter" (*Journal of Discourses* 6:276). As he said on another occasion, our work "is a work of the present. *The salvation we are seeking is for the present, and sought correctly, it can be obtained, and be continually enjoyed.* If it continues today, it is upon the same principle that it will continue tomorrow, the next day, the next week, or the next year, and, we might say, the next eternity" (*Journal of Discourses* 1:131; emphasis added).

It has been my privilege for many years to work with the youth of the Church as a seminary teacher, an institute director, and a professor of religion at Brigham Young University. I have no question but that God has reserved many of his noblest sons and daughters for this final dispensation. They are indeed a generation of excellence as well as a generation of destiny. They will do much to prepare the earth for the second coming of the Son of Man. I know them well enough to know that on the whole they want the message of the gospel straight and undiluted, that gospel games and entertainment, though fun for a brief season, soon lose their appeal to these youth. I believe this generation of youth are more pointed to Christ and the plan of redemption than any other group of young people in history. I sense keenly that they need a vision of the distant goal toward which to point themselves.

But they also need spiritual reinforcement and the fruits of their faith in the here and now. It is one thing to be able to promise a priest or a Laurel that if they remain morally clean and obey God's other laws they will be worthy of the celestial kingdom; it is another thing to assure them that if they live God's laws, including the law of chastity, they will enjoy peace and happiness and the endowments of the Holy Ghost in this life.

PRIDE OR HOPE?

We must guard against all forms of pride or self-assurance, but we must also avoid the kind of false modesty or doubt that is antithetical to faith. As Joseph Smith taught, doubt—which certainly includes a constant worry as to our standing before God or our capacity to go where Christ is—cannot coexist with saving faith. Fear and doubt "preclude the possibility of the exercise of faith in [God] for life and salvation" (*Lectures on Faith* 4:13; see also 3:20–21; 6:12).

If indeed "happiness is the object and design of our existence" (*Teachings of the Prophet Joseph Smith,* p. 255), then happiness is something to be enjoyed in the present, in the here and now, not something reserved for the distant there and then. *"If we are saved,"* President Young declared, *"we are happy,* we are filled with light, glory, intelligence, and we pursue a course to enjoy the blessings that the Lord has in store for us. If we continue to pursue that course, it produces just the thing we want, that is, *to be saved at this present moment. And this will lay the foundation to be saved forever and forever, which will amount to an eternal salvation"* (*Journal of Discourses* 1:131; emphasis added).

Living in a state of salvation does not entail an

inordinate self-confidence, but rather a hope in Christ. To hope in our modern world is to wish—or perhaps to worry or fret about some particular outcome. In the scriptures, however, hope is expectation, anticipation, and assurance. Faith in Christ, true faith, always gives rise to hope in Christ.

"And what is it that ye shall hope for? Behold I say unto you that ye shall have hope through the atonement of Christ and the power of his resurrection, to be raised unto life eternal" (Moroni 7:41).

To have faith in Christ is to have the assurance that as we rely wholly upon his merits and mercy, as we trust in his redeeming grace, we will make it (see 2 Nephi 31:19; Moroni 6:4). He will not only bridge the chasm between the ideal and the real, and thus provide that final spiritual boost into eternal life, but he will also extend to us that marvelous enabling power so essential to daily living, a power that enables us to conquer weakness and acquire the divine nature.

Living in a state of salvation is living in the quiet assurance that God is in his heaven, that Christ is the Lord, and that the plan of redemption is real and in active operation in our personal lives. It is not to be totally free of weakness, but to proceed confidently in the Savior's promise that in him we shall find strength to overcome, in him we shall find rest and peace, both here and hereafter.

Our Heavenly Father loves all of his children and is no respecter of persons. He does not love those who guide the destiny of the Church any more than he loves those who constitute the rank and file of the Church. The gifts of God, including the gift of salvation or eternal life, are freely available to all of us.

Let me share a personal experience that illustrates how much the Lord is personally interested in each of us. While serving as a bishop a number of years ago, I came upon a problem that caused me much unrest. My elders quorum president was moving. My Primary president was moving. My Relief Society president had served faithfully and well for a time and needed to be released to spend more time with her family. My Young Women president was pregnant, and because she had had so much difficulty with previous pregnancies (spending weeks in bed), she felt it would be wise to be released.

One Saturday morning I jumped in the car and set out for a city some four hours away. I was traveling to a church in that area where I would meet with seminary students and teachers for an all-day Church Education System activity.

After listening to general conference tapes and to the Tabernacle Choir for about two hours, I decided

CHAPTER 6

All Are Alike unto God

to spend some time pondering about how to reorganize and staff the ward. I reflected on how faithful my leaders had been and how much I would miss their strength and commitment. I smiled as I reminisced about the call of the Young Women president. It had been a real arm-wrestling match to get Betty Johnson to accept the call. She had said to us (the bishopric) at the time we extended the call that she was not a "youth person," that she had a young family, that she would rather do just about anything than this. More than an hour later she finally agreed to try it for a few months. As I looked back, I saw that she truly had done a remarkable job during the year she had served.

I found myself talking aloud to the Lord in prayer. "Let's start with the Relief Society. Who is it that thou hast prepared to serve as the Relief Society president?" A thought came into my mind, "You must call Betty Johnson." I shook my head, frowned, and said "No. Let's try this again. Who should be called as the president of the Relief Society?" And as quick as a flash the thought returned, this time with a bit more oomph, "You are to call Betty Johnson." I knew at that point that my connection with the Lord was out of whack and that my good intentions of getting some Church work done on the trip were about to come to naught. I dropped the whole matter and put the tapes back on.

After a very long day I headed home; it was

nearly midnight. I decided to try my hand with the Lord again; if nothing else it might help me stay awake for the long drive. I asked, "Heavenly Father, who should be called as president of the Relief Society?" For the third time I heard the words, "You are to call Betty Johnson." By now I sensed that I was pressing my luck and that maybe I shouldn't ask again. My mind raced. Betty had been the Young Women president for a year. She had requested a release because of health problems during pregnancy. She needed the time. But in spite of rational objections the feelings were strong. I tossed and turned in bed during much of the short night after I got home.

After the block of Sunday meetings the next day, I found myself in the outer office with my financial clerk, Fred Johnson, Betty's husband. After we had completed our work with the tithing, I walked out into the foyer and sat on the couch next to Betty. She was waiting for Fred. She sweetly smiled, reached over and squeezed my hand, and said, "Bishop, thanks for being sensitive about my situation. I know it isn't easy to make a change like this, but I deeply appreciate your willingness to release me."

I looked into her eyes, tried to smile, and uttered a weak, "You're welcome." I ached inside. I sensed that something needed to be done, in spite of existing problematic circumstances. I walked to the outside door of the church with the couple and found myself saying to her, "Betty, would you please do something for me?"

"Of course."

"Would you pray about what the Lord would now have you do in the ward? And when you receive a revelation, would you call me?"

She laughed aloud. "Bishop, I don't get revelations like that. I'm just a simple member of the Church."

> **IF GOD WILL BLESS A REPENTANT OLD, SMOKING, SWEARING POOL PLAYER, DON'T YOU THINK HE WILL YOU?**

"I know you feel that way," I answered, "but if you do receive a revelation, will you call me?"

She nodded. The look in her eyes made me feel rotten; I felt as though I were playing "Guess What's on My Mind."

I didn't think much about her situation the rest of that day. The phone rang early the next morning. It was for me. "Bishop, this is Betty. I need to see you right away." She then uttered a sentence in which she used a word I don't think I've ever heard before. She said, "I've had an *unearthing* night." I agreed to meet her at the institute building at 1:00 P.M.

She knocked on my door a few minutes early. Betty was a very lovely person who was always dressed impeccably. But now she stood in the framework of the door with a disheveled look—hair in her eyes, mascara stains on her face, wearing jeans and sweatshirt—holding her journal under her arm. After she had come into my office and sat down, she glared at me with an almost venomous look and said, "You did that, didn't you?"

"I don't understand what you mean. What did I do?" I asked.

"You made me have that dream."

"What dream?"

Betty then described a dream in which she found herself in our stake high council room, sitting opposite the stake president, his first counselor, and me. In the dream she was called to serve in a particular position in the ward.

"What was the calling?" I inquired.

"I don't want to talk about it!" she shot back.

After two more attempts to get her to admit what the calling was, I said, "You were being called as the ward Relief Society president, weren't you?"

She nodded and then wept. "Bishop Millet, you know this is the only way I could have been persuaded to accept this heavy responsibility, don't you?"

I nodded. "Will you do it?" I asked.

Betty answered that she would do the best she could. She then asked me why I was sitting with the stake presidency in the dream, and I stated that I supposed the dream was merely an indication that she was being called by those in authority.

A few days after Betty was sustained (and after she had calmed down appreciably), she commented to me: "You know, I have always considered myself to be an average member of the Church. I have a testimony of the gospel. I know that the Lord guides the Church and its leaders, and I have always believed that visions or dreams are real but basically reserved for the apostles and prophets. It feels good to know that the Lord can even work through simple people like Betty Johnson."

Betty was a remarkable Relief Society president and had very few problems with her pregnancy. She gained the respect of the sisters very quickly. Though shy by nature, she spoke with a confidence born of a conviction that she had been called of God. By the way, as part of "the rest of the story," it is interesting to note that, just as Betty had seen in her dream, I was called to serve as a counselor to the stake president several weeks later!

God loves Betty Johnson and all of the Betty Johnsons throughout the earth, and there is no reward reserved for prophets that is not available to each one of us. We can make it.

EAGER TO ACCEPT OUR OFFERINGS

Elder Jeffrey R. Holland of the Quorum of the Twelve has written of another example of God's love, patience, and eagerness to accept the offerings of the weak and the simple:

"The Brethren used to announce at general conference the names of those who had been called on missions. Not only was this the way friends and neighbors learned of the call, but more often than not it was the way the missionary learned of it as well. One such prospect was Eli H. Pierce. A railroad man by trade, he had not been very faithful in the Church. . . . His mind had been given totally to what he demurely called 'temporalities.' He said he had never read more than a few pages of scripture in his life, that he had spoken at only one public gathering (an effort that he says 'was no credit' to himself or those who heard him), and he used the vernacular of the railroad and barroom with a finesse born of long practice. He bought cigars wholesale—a thousand at a time—and he regularly lost his paycheck playing pool. . . .

"Well, the Lord knew what Eli Pierce was and he knew something else. He knew what Eli Pierce could become. When the call came that October 5, 1875, Eli wasn't even in the Tabernacle. He was out working on one of the railroad lines. A fellow employee, once he had recovered from the shock of it all, ran out to telegraph the startling news. Brother Pierce writes: 'At the very moment this intelligence was being flashed over the wires, I was sitting lazily thrown back in an office rocking chair, my feet on the desk, reading a novel and simultaneously sucking on an old Dutch pipe just to vary the monotony of cigar smoking. As soon as I had been informed of what had taken place, I threw the novel in the waste basket, the pipe in the corner (and have never touched either to this hour). I sent in my resignation . . . to take effect at once, in order that I might have time for study and preparation. I then started into town to buy [scripture].'

"Then Eli wrote these stirring words: 'Remarkable as it may seem, and has since appeared to me, a thought of disregarding the call, or of refusing to comply with the requirement, never once entered my mind. The only question I asked—and I asked it a thousand times—was: How can I accomplish this mission? How can I, who am so shamefully ignorant and untaught in doctrine, do honor to God and justice to the souls of men, and merit the trust reposed in me by the Priesthood?'

"With such genuine humility fostering resolution rather than defeating it, Eli Pierce fulfilled a remarkable mission. His journal could appropriately close on a completely renovated life with this one line: 'Throughout our entire mission we were greatly blessed.' But I add one experience to make the point.

"During the course of his missionary service, Brother Pierce was called in to administer to the infant child of a branch president whom he knew and loved.

> MUCH OF OUR DISCOURAGEMENT STEMS FROM OUR INABILITY TO RELY ON THE LORD AND TRUST IN HIM.

Unfortunately the wife of the branch president had become embittered and now seriously objected to any religious activity within the home, including a blessing for this dying child. With the mother refusing to leave the bedside and the child too ill to move, the humble branch president with his missionary friend Eli retired to a small upper room in the house to pray for the baby's life. The mother, suspecting just such an act, sent one of the older children to observe and report back.

"There in that secluded chamber the two men knelt and prayed fervently until, in Brother Pierce's own words, 'we felt that the child would live and knew that our prayers had been heard.' Arising from their knees, they turned slowly only to see the young girl standing in the partially open doorway gazing intently into the room. She seemed, however, quite oblivious to the movements of the two men. She stood entranced for some seconds, her eyes immovable. Then she said, 'Papa, who was that man in there?' Her father said, 'That is Brother Pierce. You know him.' 'No,' she said matter-of-factly, 'I mean the *other* man.' 'There was no other, darling, except Brother Pierce and myself. We were praying for the baby.' 'Oh, there was another man,' the child insisted, 'for I saw him standing [above] you and Brother Pierce and he was dressed in white.' Now if God in his heavens will do that for a repentant old cigar-smoking, inactive, stern-swearing pool player, don't you think he'll do it for you? He will if your resolve is as deep and permanent as Eli Pierce's. In the Church we ask for faith, not infallibility" (*However Long and Hard the Road,* pp. 7–9).

Blessings for "Common People"

Elder Boyd K. Packer once spoke of a man who, though not directly related to me, demonstrated a principle that touches my soul: "Whenever we seek for true testimony we come, finally, to ordinary men and women and children. Let me quote from the diary of Joseph Millett, a little-known missionary of an earlier time.

"Joseph Millett, with his large family, was suffering through very, very difficult times. He wrote in his journal: 'One of my children came in and said that Brother Newton Hall's folks was out of bread, had none that day. I divided our flour in a sack to send up to Brother Hall. Just then Brother Hall came. Says I, "Brother Hall, are you out of flour?" "Brother Millett, we have none." "Well, Brother Hall, there is some in that sack. I have divided and was going to send it to you. Your children told mine that you was out." Brother Hall began to cry. He said he had tried others, but could not get any. He went to the cedars and prayed to the Lord, and the Lord told him to go to Joseph Millett. "Well, Brother Hall, you needn't bring this back. If the Lord sent you for it you don't owe me for it."'

"That night Joseph Millett recorded a remarkable

sentence in his journal: 'You can't tell me how good it made me feel to know that the Lord knew there was such a person as Joseph Millett.' The Lord knew Joseph Millett. And He knows all those men and women like him, and they are many. Theirs are the lives that are most worth recording" (in *Conference Report*, April 1980, p. 84).

As I have counseled over the years with many members of the Church, good people who hope against hope that one day they might somehow qualify for a kingdom of glory, I sense among some of them the feeling that they must either be called to high position or perform some extraordinary service in order to be saved. This is simply not true. As President Joseph F. Smith taught, "To do well those things which God ordained to be the common lot of all mankind, is the truest greatness" (*Gospel Doctrine*, p. 285). Quietly living the gospel, rearing a family, teaching them the gospel, magnifying our callings in the Church, reaching out to others in quiet acts of Christian service, letting the Spirit of Christ shape our basic nature and direct our steps—these are the things out of which a celestial character is molded and the things that prepare us for entrance into everlasting life with Gods and angels.

"[You] don't need to get a complex," Elder Bruce R. McConkie declared, "or get a feeling that you have to be perfect to be saved. You don't. . . . What you have to do is get on the straight and narrow path—thus charting a course leading to eternal life—and then, being on that path, pass out of this life in full fellowship. I'm not saying that you don't have to keep the commandments. I'm saying you don't have to be perfect to be saved. If you did, no one would be saved. . . . If you're on that path and pressing forward, and you die, you'll never get off the path. There is no such thing as falling off the straight and narrow path in the life to come, and the reason is that this life is the time that is given to men to prepare for eternity. Now is the time and the day of your salvation, so if you're working zealously in this life—though you haven't fully overcome the world and you haven't done all you hoped you might do—you're still going to be saved. You don't have to do what Jacob said, 'Go beyond the mark.' You don't have to live a life that's truer than true. You don't have to have an excessive zeal that becomes fanatical and becomes unbalancing. What you have to do is stay in the mainstream of the Church and live as upright and decent people live in the Church. . . . If you're on that path when death comes—because this is the time and the day appointed, this is the probationary estate—you'll never fall off from it, and, for all practical purposes, your calling and election is made sure" ("The Probationary Test of Mortality," pp. 12–13).

> JESUS IS OUR SAVIOR, AND HE NOT ONLY CAN SAVE US BUT HE YEARNS TO DO SO.

A Cause for Rejoicing

We must have hope. We must have rejoicing. If any people in all the wide world have reason to be positive, to rejoice and exult in blessings unmeasured and graces abounding, it is the Latter-day Saints. If any religious body in all of creation ever had reason to look forward to the future, to prepare with joyful anticipation for that which is yet to be, it is the members of the restored Church. I am convinced that much of the discouragement that exists in the hearts and minds of many Latter-day Saints may be traced to their inability to rely on the Lord and trust in his mercies.

To be sure, we need to do all we can to prove ourselves worthy of the Lord's goodness (and to keep our part of the gospel covenant). But we must also accept the revealed verity that when we have done all we can—when we have stretched to the limit, have placed our offerings on the altar of faith, no matter how meager they may seem to us at the time—we then have done what was asked of us and we will come to know that the Lord is pleased with us. As Elder Neal A. Maxwell has counseled us, "We can allow for the reality that God is still more concerned with growth than with geography" (*Notwithstanding My Weakness*, p. 11). The Lord's gentle commendation to a little-known man named Oliver Granger is equally applicable to us: "When he falls he shall rise again, for his sacrifice shall be more sacred unto me than his increase, saith the Lord" (D&C 117:13).

Jesus is our Savior, and he not only can save us but he yearns to do so. He loves us, one and all. This I know. While the father of all lies seeks to dissuade and discourage, Christ our Lord extends his arm of mercy to us all the day long. He seeks to seal us to him everlastingly. I am persuaded that we not only can make it but that we will make it, if we stay on course, stay in covenant, and stay in tune with the Spirit of the Lord. "And may the Lord bless you, and keep your garments spotless, that ye may at last be brought to sit down with Abraham, Isaac, and Jacob, and the holy prophets who have been ever since the world began, having your garments spotless even as their garments are spotless, in the kingdom of heaven to go no more out" (Alma 7:25).

Early in this work I shared an experience I had in 1976 while listening to Elder Bruce R. McConkie. His words to Church educators—"You tell your students that far more of our Father's children will be exalted than we think!"—sent my mind reeling then, and the deeper implications of that message drive much of what I feel, do, and teach today.

Epilogue

No one who reads this small book should misunderstand what I am trying to say. I do not believe men and women will be exalted who come into the Church and then set at naught the counsels of God or ignore the prophetic direction of the living oracles. I do not believe the celestial kingdom will have people within it who with malicious intent violate the laws of God and trample under their feet spiritual things. But I do believe that the children of God who receive the ordinances of salvation and then seek with all their might to keep their promises and remain in covenant—even though they may have been far from perfect along the way and as they passed through death—will go into paradise, continue to progress and develop and improve, and eventually enjoy celestial, resurrected glory.

I am deeply moved by some of the lessons from the lives of great people of scripture. In the Book of

Mormon, for example, Nephi, son of Lehi, was consummately righteous, a person of unusual faith. "My soul delighteth in the things of the Lord," he wrote, "and my heart pondereth continually upon the things which I have seen and heard." Now that's the Nephi we all know and love, the man without guile, the solid, steadfast defender of the truth. But notice what follows: "Nevertheless, notwithstanding the great goodness of the Lord, in showing me his great and marvelous works, my heart exclaimeth: *O wretched man that I am! Yea, my heart sorroweth because of my flesh; my soul grieveth because of mine iniquities. I am encompassed about, because of the temptations and the sins which do so easily beset me*" (2 Nephi 4:16–18; emphasis added). Wait a minute! we shout. What happened to our hero? What happened to the holy man who delights in the things of God? Answer: The same Nephi who communed with God regularly, had visions and dreams, and penetrated the veil often—that same Nephi wrestled with the flesh, with his humanness, with a fallen mortal nature.

Let's take a second case study, this from the opening chapters of the book of Mosiah. The people of Benjamin were summoned to a great covenant-renewal ceremony to receive a benedictory address from their remarkable king. They are described as being "a diligent people in keeping the commandments of the Lord" (Mosiah 1:11). We assume they were members of the

Church, were what we would call good and faithful people. They listened as King Benjamin introduced his son Mosiah as his successor and then as he answered to the people for his stewardship with a clear conscience. Benjamin spoke of the importance of serving one another and taught the timeless lesson that when we are in the service of our fellow beings we are only in the service of our God. Benjamin then quoted extensively from the words of an angel concerning the coming condescension of Jehovah, the Lord God Omnipotent; of the sufferings, death, and resurrection of the Holy One as an atoning sacrifice for all; and of the need to put off the natural man and put on Christ (Mosiah 2–3).

"And now, it came to pass that when king Benjamin had made an end of speaking the words which had been delivered unto him by the angel of the Lord, that he cast his eyes round about on the multitude, and behold they had fallen to the earth, for the fear of the Lord had come upon them." And now note this unusual statement about this diligent people: "And *they had viewed themselves in their own carnal state, even less than the dust of the earth*" (Mosiah 4:1–2; emphasis added). What? A diligent and faithful people began to see themselves as less than the dust of the earth? How so? Before we answer, let's consider another case.

As my final example, I'd like us to take a look at one of my favorite Book of Mormon personalities,

Mahonri Moriancumr, known to most of us as the brother of Jared. The Lord had commanded Jared, his brother, and their families and selected friends to leave a wicked world behind at the time of the tower of Babel and the confusion of tongues and to travel to a promised land (see Ether 1–3).

> WE CAN DEAL WITH OUR SINS AND FRAILTIES ONLY BY YIELDING TO THE CAPTAIN OF OUR SOULS.

When it came to constructing and occupying barges to cross the great deep, the Jaredites faced two significant challenges: air and light. When the brother of Jared asked the Lord for help with the problem of ventilation, the Lord freely gave him specific instructions; apparently it was beyond the capacity of the brother of Jared to come up with the solution by himself. When it came to the matter of light, the Lord said, in essence, "What would you have me to do?" The brother of Jared prepared sixteen transparent stones and brought them to the Lord. He then pleaded with the Almighty to touch them, for he had sufficient faith that if they were touched by God they would shine.

The prayer of this remarkably righteous man, one whose name is forevermore enshrined in our Who's Who in Faith, is most instructive. "O Lord," he implored, "thou hast said that we must be encompassed about by the floods. Now behold, O Lord, and do not be angry with thy servant because of his weakness before thee; for we know that thou art holy and dwellest in the heavens, and that *we are unworthy before thee; because of the fall our natures have become evil continually*" (Ether 3:2; emphasis added). An evil nature within the brother of Jared? What's going on?

SAINTS WITH WEAKNESSES

In each of the foregoing scriptural illustrations, we find that godly people, men and women of faith, those that most of us would surely deem worthy of exaltation, felt the effects of the Fall and the pull of this fallen world. They were good people, noble souls, but keenly aware of their weakness. My point here is that some of the greatest men and women who have ever lived have been very aware of their weaknesses, of their limitations, of their inabilities to make it alone. They knew they were not perfect on their own. Their humility was coupled with, inextricably tied to, their trust in and reliance upon One who was perfect, One who had done all things well.

Nephi wrote: "And when I desire to rejoice, my heart groaneth because of my sins; nevertheless"—and this is a huge nevertheless—"*I know in whom I have trusted. My God hath been my support*" (2 Nephi 4:19–20; emphasis added). Likewise, the brother of Jared said in prayer: "Because of the fall our natures have become evil continually; nevertheless"—there's that word again!—"nevertheless, O Lord, *thou hast given us a commandment that we must call upon thee, that from thee we may receive according to our desires*" (Ether 3:2; emphasis added). In short, one of the only ways we can deal with our mistakes, our sins, and our frailties without giving up or surrendering to the devil is to acknowledge fully and yield completely to the Captain of our souls, Jesus Christ.

The people of Benjamin—as should we all—"cried aloud with one voice, saying: O have mercy, and apply the atoning blood of Christ that we may receive forgiveness of our sins, and our hearts may be purified; for we believe in Jesus Christ, the Son of God, who created heaven and earth, and all things." And what happened to them can and does and will happen to us, if our hearts are welded to the Holy One of Israel as were theirs: "And it came to pass that after they had spoken these words the Spirit of the Lord came upon them, and they were filled with joy, having received a remission of their sins, and having peace of conscience, because of the exceeding faith which they had in Jesus Christ" (Mosiah 4:2–3).

It is not the world's version of self-esteem, a burgeoning self-confidence, that will see us through the vexations of the soul; it is confidence in God. A proper confession of our nothingness without the Lord, linked to a total acknowledgement of his power to recover, rescue, redeem, ransom, and renew us—these things lay the foundation for hope in Christ and provide the godly optimism so needed in a depressing world. Surrender results in solace. As President Howard W. Hunter explained: "Indifference to the Savior or failure to keep the commandments of God brings about insecurity, inner turmoil, and contention. These are the opposites of peace. *Peace can come to an individual only by an unconditional surrender to him who is the Prince of peace and who has the power to confer peace*" (*That We Might Have Joy*, p. 30; emphasis added).

COME UNTO CHRIST AND HIS LOVE

Like Alma, I wish with all my heart that I had the power to "speak with the trump of God, with a voice to shake the earth" (Alma 29:1). I would bear testimony that there is a God in heaven, that he lives, and that he loves us infinitely and perfectly. I would bear witness of the good news, the glad tidings—that Jesus is the Christ, the Redeemer of all mankind, and that peace and happiness here and eternal reward hereafter are to be found only in him. I would bear pure testimony that God has spoken anew in our day through a modern prophet, Joseph Smith; that through that choice seer and his successors the doctrines of salvation and the divine powers by which men and women may truly be forgiven of sin and become new creatures in

Christ have been made available once again; and that The Church of Jesus Christ of Latter-day Saints is indeed the kingdom of God on the earth and the custodian of the fulness of the gospel of Jesus Christ.

I wish there were some way I could speak so as to be heard, from one pole of the earth to the other, in bearing a like witness that our God is gracious, slow to anger, and easy to be entreated. We are literally his children. He longs for us to return to his presence. "And now, my beloved brethren, seeing that our merciful God has given us so great knowledge concerning these things, let us remember him, and lay aside our sins, and not hang down our heads, for we are not cast off" (2 Nephi 10:20).

> PEACE CAN COME ONLY BY AN UNCONDITIONAL SURRENDER TO HIM WHO IS THE PRINCE OF PEACE.

One of the great needs in our day is for Latter-day Saints to have balance in their lives, balance between zeal in keeping the commandments and patience in achieving our goals, balance between a wholehearted devotion to truth and a loving acceptance of those (including ourselves) who fall short. And in our personal lives there needs to be a balance between a type of divine discontent—in which we are constantly striving to be better than we are—and what Nephi called a "perfect brightness of hope" (2 Nephi 31:20), which is the quiet but soul-affirming anticipation that if we trust in the

Lord and seek earnestly to do our best, he will make up the difference in time and in eternity.

In the meantime, as Elder Neal A. Maxwell has written: "We can contemplate how far we have already come in the climb along the pathway to perfection; it is usually much further than we acknowledge, and such reflections restore resolve. . . . We can know that when we have *truly* given what we have, it is like paying a full tithe; it is, in that respect, *all* that was asked. . . . Finally, we can accept this stunning, irrevocable truth: Our Lord can lift us from deep despair and cradle us midst any care. . . . This is a gospel of grand expectations, but God's grace is sufficient for each of us if we remember that there are no *instant* Christians" (*Notwithstanding My Weakness,* pp. 9–11; emphasis in original).

Life may be difficult, but it need not be discouraging. The Lord of Life "loveth the world, even that he layeth down his own life that he may draw all men unto him. Wherefore, he commandeth none that they shall not partake of his salvation.

"Behold, doth he cry unto any, saying: Depart from me? Behold I say unto you, Nay; but he saith: Come unto me all ye ends of the earth, buy milk and honey, without money and without price. . . .

"Hath he commanded any that they should not partake of his salvation? Behold I say unto you, Nay; but he hath given it free for all men; and he hath commanded his people that they should persuade all men to repentance.

"Behold, hath the Lord commanded any that they should not partake of his goodness? Behold I say unto you, Nay; but all men are privileged the one like unto the other, and none are forbidden" (2 Nephi 26:24–25, 27–28).

Like Ammon, I feel to rejoice in God's matchless goodness and mercy. "Therefore, let us glory, yea, we will glory in the Lord; yea, we will rejoice, for our joy is full; yea, we will praise our God forever. Behold, who can glory too much in the Lord? Yea, who can say too much of his great power, and of his mercy, and of his long-suffering towards the children of men? Behold, I say unto you, I cannot say the smallest part which I feel" (Alma 26:16).

The Divine Redeemer's eternal invitation has been extended to each of us. He knows us, one and all. He knows where we have succeeded and where we have fallen short, and yet he invites us into fellowship with him and with the Father. It is my prayer that we may respond affirmatively and actively and thereby "come unto Christ, and be perfected in him" (Moroni 10:32).

BIBLIOGRAPHY

Cannon, George Q. *Gospel Truth*. Salt Lake City: Deseret
    Book Co., 1987.

------. "Discourse." *Millennial Star*, vol. 56, 1894.

Hafen, Bruce C. *The Broken Heart*. Salt Lake City:
    Deseret Book Co., 1989.

Holland, Jeffrey R. *However Long and Hard the Road*. Salt
    Lake City: Deseret Book Co., 1985.

Hunter, Howard W. *That We Might Have Joy*. Salt Lake
    City: Deseret Book Co., 1994.

Lewis, C. S. *Mere Christianity*. New York: Macmillan,
    1952.

MacArthur, John F., Jr. *Faith Works: The Gospel According
    to the Apostles*. Dallas: Word Publishing, 1993.

------. *The Gospel According to Jesus*. Rev. ed. Grand
    Rapids: Zondervan Publishing House, 1994.

Maxwell, Neal A. *Notwithstanding My Weakness*. Salt
    Lake City: Deseret Book Co., 1981.

McConkie, Bruce R. "Discourse." In *Conference Report*.
    Salt Lake City: The Church of Jesus Christ of Latter-
    day Saints, October 1976.

------. *Doctrinal New Testament Commentary*. 3 vols.
    Salt Lake City: Bookcraft, 1965–73.

------. "Jesus Christ and Him Crucified." *1976*

Devotional Speeches of the Year. Provo, Utah: Brigham Young University Press, 1977.

———. *Mormon Doctrine.* 2d ed. Salt Lake City: Bookcraft, 1966.

———. "The Probationary Test of Mortality." Address to the Salt Lake Institute of Religion, 10 January 1982.

———. "The Seven Deadly Heresies." *1980 Devotional Speeches of the Year.* Provo, Utah: Brigham Young University Press, 1980.

Millet, Robert L. *Christ-Centered Living.* Salt Lake City: Bookcraft, 1994.

———. *Steadfast and Immovable: Striving for Spiritual Maturity.* Salt Lake City: Deseret Book Co., 1992.

Packer, Boyd K. "Discourses." In *Conference Report.* Salt Lake City: The Church of Jesus Christ of Latter-day Saints, April 1980, April 1992.

———. *The Holy Temple.* Salt Lake City: Bookcraft, 1980.

Pratt, Orson. "The Holy Spirit." In *Orson Pratt: Writings of an Apostle.* Salt Lake City: Mormon Heritage Publishers, 1976.

Robinson, Stephen E. *Believing Christ.* Salt Lake City: Deseret Book Co., 1992.

Smith, Joseph. *Lectures on Faith.* Salt Lake City: Deseret Book Co., 1971.

———. *Teachings of the Prophet Joseph Smith.* comp. Joseph Fielding Smith. Salt Lake City: Deseret Book Co., 1976.

Smith, Joseph F. *Gospel Doctrine.* Salt Lake City: Deseret
    Book Co., 1971.

Sperry, Sidney B. *Paul's Life and Letters.* Salt Lake City:
    Bookcraft, 1955.

Young, Brigham. *Journal of Discourses.* 26 vols.
    Liverpool: F. D. Richards & Sons, 1855–86.

INDEX

Gifts, spiritual, 63–67
Grace, 50, 68–69
Granger, Oliver, 99–100
Guiltlessness through Christ, 42–43

Happiness, 85
Holland, Jeffrey R., story by, 92–96
Holy Ghost: as Comforter, 33–35; as Sanctifier, 45, 53–54, 64; as
    Holy Spirit of Promise, 51; as Revelator, 64; companionship of,
    77–82
Hope, 6, 85–86
Humility, 49, 102–6

Jared, brother of. *See* Moriancumr, Mahonri
Jesus Christ: knowing, 2; faith in, 6, 85–86, 102–6; fix eyes on, 7;
    as Redeemer, 27–29; personal presence of, 37; justification
    through, 40–46; grace of, 50, 68–69; covenant with, 68–69;
    mercy of, 110
Job, 60
John the Revelator, vision of, 19–20
Johnson, Betty, 89–92
Justification, 26; types of, 39–40; through Christ, 40–46; retaining,
    48–50

Lehi, 28; dream of, 18–19

Marriage, temple, 51
McConkie, Bruce R., on charting course to eternal life, 10–17,
    97–98
Mercy, 43, 110
Millennium, 12
Millett, Joseph, 96–97
Missionary experiences, 30–34, 46–47
Moriancumr, Mahonri, 28, 104–6

Nephi, 102, 105
Noah and sons, 59

Obedience. *See* Covenants, keeping